Drama Links:
Teaching Drama within the English Framework

Larraine Harrison

Hodder & Stoughton

A MEMBER OF THE HODDER HEADLINE GROUP

ACKNOWLEDGEMENTS

The author would like to thank the English departments of Royston High School and The Priory School in Barnsley, for their advice on suitable texts, and Kate and Martyn Harrison for their technical and editorial support during the writing of this book.

Copyright Text:
p96 an extract from *Goodnight Mr Tom* by Michelle Magorian (Kestrel, 1981) © Michelle Magorian, 1981; pp99–100 extracts from *Stone Cold* by Robert Swindells (Hamish Hamilton, 1993) © Robert Swindells, 1993; pp103 and 128 extracts from *Holes* by Louis Sachar. Reproduced by kind permission of Bloomsbury Publishers; p111 *Digging* from *Opened Ground* by Seamus Heaney. Reproduced by permission of Faber and Faber Ltd; p112 *My Hero* by Willis Hall from *Spooky Rhymes* © Willis Hall, Productions Ltd 1987. First published by Egmont Books Limited, London and used with permission; p113 *Lullaby* by Rosemary Norman, from *I Wouldn't Thank you for a Valentine,* Viking, 1992. Reproduced by kind permission of the author; p114 *Catrin* from *Collected Poems* by Gillian Clarke. Reproduced by permission of Carcanet Press Limited; p114 *Poem* from *Kid* by Simon Armitage. Reproduced by permission of Faber and Faber Ltd; pp120–122 an extract from *The Switch* by Anthony Horowitz © 1996. Reproduced by permission of the publisher Walker Books Limited, London; p127 an extract from *The Hobbit* by J.R.R Tolkien. Reproduced by kind permission of HarperCollins Publishers Ltd; p129 an extract from *The Village Dinosaur* by Phyllis Arkle. Reproduced by kind permission of Hodder and Stoughton Limited; p130 an extract from *Playing on the Edge* by Neil Arksey (Puffin, 2000) © Neil Arksey, 2000; p132 an extract from *About Face* by Paul Whitfield from *Cracking Drama KS3 Scripts,* NATE, Sheffield, 2001. Reproduced by kind permission of the author; p133 *Harry Pushed Her* by Peter Thabit Jones © Peter Thabit Jones, 2002; p136 an extract from *The Canterbury Tales* by Geraldine McCaughrean. Reproduced by kind permission of Oxford University Press; pp137–138 an extract from *The Canterbury Tales* by Geoffrey Chaucer, translated by Nevill Coghill (Penguin Classics 1951, fourth revised edition 1977) Copyright 1951 by Nevill Coghill © the Estate of Nevill Coghill, 1958, 1960, 1975, 1977; pp140–141 an extract from *Dicing with Death* by Simon Adorian, Nelson, 1999. Reproduced by permission of Nelson Thornes Ltd.; p147 *The Ballad of Charlotte Dymond* by Charles Causley from *Collected Poems.* Reproduced by permission of the author and David Higham Associates.

Copyright Artwork/Photographs:
pp41, 105, 107–110, 135 © Zhenya Matysiak; p98 Evacuees arriving at their billet (1939) © Popperfoto.

Every effort has been made to trace copyright holders of material reproduced in this book. Any rights not acknowledged will be acknowledged in subsequent printings if notice is given to the publisher.

Orders: please contact Bookpoint Ltd, 130 Milton Park, Abingdon, Oxon OX14 4SB. Telephone: (44) 01235 827720, Fax: (44) 01235 400454. Lines are open from 9.00–6.00, Monday to Saturday, with a 24 hour message answering service. Email address: orders@bookpoint.co.uk

British Library Cataloguing in Publication Data
A catalogue record for this title is available from The British Library

ISBN 0 340 84654 2

First published 2002
Impression number   10 9 8 7 6 5 4 3 2 1
Year   2008 2007 2006 2005 2004 2003 2002

Copyright © 2002 Larraine Harrison

Cover illustration from Michael Stones.
Typeset by Fakenham Photosetting Limited, Fakenham, Norfolk
Printed in Great Britain for Hodder & Stoughton Educational, a division of Hodder Headline Plc, 338 Euston Road, London NW1 3BH by Hobbs The Printers, Totton, Hampshire.

CONTENTS

· ·

INTRODUCTION

Five years ago, in a shop in my local town, I met a young man I used to teach in Year 10. He said to me:

'Do you remember when we were all trapped in that submarine Miss, and Michaela read out her poem and we all cried?'

I did remember. It was one of those magical moments when I had used drama to motivate and stimulate poetry writing for a group of less than enthusiastic adolescents, and it had moved us all to tears.

It was one of those defining moments, when all the composing, drafting, editing and final writing of that poem achieved the ultimate aim of all poetry: to touch the emotions of the reader. This incident reinforced my belief that when drama is linked to English, it has the potential to create effective and sometimes memorable English lessons that stay with pupils long after they have left school. Of course, not all lessons achieve these heights, but good drama has high motivational value and holds within it the power to develop pupils' interior visualisation, analysis and appreciation of texts.

Drama is part of pupils' entitlement in the National Curriculum for English, and the current Framework for English at Key Stage 3 contains a number of detailed drama objectives for each year group. Many schools unfortunately no longer have drama departments, leaving the responsibility for drama at the door of the English department. Schools who do have drama departments may be tempted to rely on their drama teachers to teach all the required drama objectives in the English Framework. However, it would seem counterproductive to deny English teachers the opportunity to access such a powerful teaching tool in their attempts to raise standards in English and literacy. Good practice would seem to be where drama departments work with English departments to construct joint medium-term plans for drama at Key Stage 3, based on the drama objectives in the English Framework.

Some English teachers have been successfully utilising the potential of drama as a learning medium for many years. However, many teachers still remain unsure about how to incorporate drama into English lessons and, consequently, remain unaware of its full potential as a powerful and effective teaching method.

This book is designed to help English teachers make effective links between the drama objectives and other key objectives in the English Framework. In so doing it is hoped that teachers will enable pupils to make good progress in both English and drama, via powerful and effective teaching methods.

The strategies in this book have been selected as those most appropriate for teachers who have relatively little experience of using drama within English lessons. The instructions and explanations are written in considerable detail to support the most inexperienced teacher. Teachers with more experience can easily adapt the details to suit their own needs. Ideas for drama lessons are also included where appropriate, to support English teachers who are timetabled to teach drama but lack confidence and expertise.

The material is organised into 10 units; each representing a different drama strategy. These 10 strategies have been selected to support teachers who wish to build up their confidence in drama teaching, and as such do not represent an exhaustive list. The Further Reading section is provided for those teachers who wish to extend their repertoire of strategies and increase their knowledge and understanding of drama. Each unit contains detailed examples of how to apply the strategy in Years 7, 8 and 9. The examples are all presented as English Framework literacy lessons and some also as drama lessons. All the literacy lessons are designed to take place within the English classroom, without the need to move the furniture. Every example, whether it be a literacy lesson or a drama lesson, is closely linked to the English Framework drama objectives, and includes links to other objectives where appropriate. Most examples also include a writing task or contain links to writing, and many are centred around a specific text.

The detailed examples within this book are designed to encourage teachers and pupils to engage in drama with discipline, integrity, reflection and enjoyment. If drama is about making meaning, then we need to harness its power to motivate pupils to speak, listen, read and write. Drama links with many aspects of English, including reading for meaning and the content and structure of pupils' writing. Whenever I am asked to comment on potential links between drama and English, I remember Michaela, who uncharacteristically spent a large amount of time composing and drafting her poem for the forthcoming drama. I then recall the moment in the submarine, when she read out her poem with a conviction that moved us to tears. This book is underpinned by a conviction that all English teachers can be supported to raise standards of literacy through integrating drama into their lessons, and making links between the drama objectives and other key objectives in the English Framework.

Explanation of Icons and Objectives

Icons
The following icons are used throughout the book:

When you see this ...	It represents ...
	Links to the National Curriculum Key Stages 3 and 4 English Programmes of Study
(FW)	Links to the English Framework Objectives
	Links to Schemes of Work
	Links to specific texts

Objectives
The Key Stage 3 English Framework Objectives are coded in this book as follows:

Code used ...	What this represents ...
Wd	Word Level
Sn	Sentence Level
TLR	Text Level – Reading
TLW	Text Level – Writing
S&L	Speaking and Listening

ASSESSMENT

It is not the intention of this book to suggest that English teachers spend large amounts of time filling in detailed assessment sheets on pupils' progress in drama. However, some degree of assessment is necessary to track pupils' progress through the drama objectives in the English Framework. The Further Reading section of this book includes publications such as *Cracking Drama* by NATE Drama Committee and *Beginning Drama 11–14* by Jonothon Neelands, which cover the assessment of, and progression in drama in some depth. Suffice it to say here, that for assessment to be formative, English teachers need to be able to recognise the main areas of progression in drama. These areas can be broadly defined as:

- knowledge and understanding of drama techniques and genres
- application of drama techniques to make meanings
- collaboration with others to create and shape the drama
- reflection and response to drama, as participants and as an audience
- critical evaluation of drama as participants and as an audience.

Pupils also need to be made aware of these areas, in order to evaluate their own progress in drama, as defined in the objectives.

Teachers may assess progress in drama through:

- systematic observation of groups of pupils on a rota basis
- discussion with groups of pupils, live or on tape
- photographic or video evidence
- scrutiny of individual pupils' work, such as play scripts, drama logs, imaginative writing, reflective artwork / diagrams / notes and written evaluations.

Mapping Grid for the English Framework Drama Objectives

OBJECTIVES	UNITS									
SPEAKING AND LISTENING: DRAMA	1	2	3	4	5	6	7	8	9	10
Year 7										
S&L 15	●	●	●		●	●				●
S&L 16							●	●	●	●
S&L 17					●					●
S&L 18	●	●	●	●						●
S&L 19								●		●
Year 8										
S&L 13								●		●
S&L 14	●									●
S&L 15	●	●	●	●	●				●	●
S&L 16						●	●	●		●
Year 9										
S&L 11								●		●
S&L 12	●	●	●	●	●	●			●	●
S&L 13	●				●					
S&L 14						●	●	●		●
S&L 15								●		

Please see individual units for links to other English Framework objectives.

UNIT ONE   FREEZE-FRAMES, THOUGHT TRACKING AND FORUM THEATRE

Making Links

Links to the National Curriculum Key Stages 3 and 4 English Programmes of Study

Drama: **S&L 4**   To participate in a range of drama activities and to evaluate their own and others' contributions, pupils should be taught to use a variety of dramatic techniques to explore ideas, issues, texts and meanings.

Links to the English Framework Objectives:

Year 7
Drama: **S&L 15, 18**
Reading for meaning: **TLR 8**
Understanding the author's craft: **TLR 14, 16**
Imagine, explore, entertain: **TLW 9**

Year 8
Drama: **S&L 14, 15**
Reading for meaning: **TLR 6**
Persuade, argue, advise: **TLW 13**

Year 9
Drama: **S&L 12, 13**
Study of literary texts: **TLR 14**
Inform, explain, describe: **TLW 11**

Links to Schemes of Work

The Novel; Writing in role; Bias in the news; Shakespeare

Links to specific texts

Year 7   *Goodnight Mr Tom* by Michelle Magorian
Year 8   *Stone Cold* by Robert Swindells
Year 9   *Macbeth* Act 3 Scene 4 and Act 4 Scene 1 by William Shakespeare

Definitions

Freeze-frame – a significant moment from a text is frozen in time and depicted by a group of pupils. This is also known as a still image and can be compared to the effect created by pressing the pause button on a video.

Thought tracking – pupils in a freeze-frame express their characters' thoughts. This is sometimes referred to as *speaking thoughts*.

Forum theatre – the class make the key decisions about the freeze-frame, based on evidence from the text.

Teaching and Learning Rationale

The combined strategies of freeze-frame, thought tracking and forum theatre help develop pupils' skills of inference and deduction, whilst also catering for those pupils who learn best through visual and kinaesthetic teaching styles. These strategies are appropriate for a literacy lesson or a drama lesson. However, when applied in a particular way during a literacy lesson, they provide a context for writing, and can help pupils improve their reading and writing skills through exploring the impact of powerful writing on the reader and identifying authorial intent.

These strategies can be utilised to support writing by taking pupils through the following three stages:

1 Visualise and Analyse → 2 Respond and Communicate → 3 Draft and Write

1 Visualise and Analyse

The freeze-frame provides a visual focus for discussion and analysis of texts. It works to stimulate pupils' interior visualisation of text, by clawing a moment from a page and making it tangible. Once pupils can see the moment depicted, they are better able to speculate on the feelings of the characters and discuss the issues involved. They are also more inclined to search through the text for evidence to justify their views. In addition, if the freeze-frame is preceded by an opportunity for the pupils to make a personal response to the text in terms of what they imagine they can see, feel, sense and connect as they read the passage, this will feed the freeze-frame analysis and contribute to the planning of subsequent pieces of writing.

2 Respond and Communicate

The discussion about the thoughts and feelings of the characters in the freeze-frame form a model for pupils to formulate their own responses in role as eye-witnesses or characters. Pupils' individual responses are further reinforced and developed when they are given the opportunity to communicate their initial responses to other pupils.

3 Draft and Write

Pupils are now in a position to draw on what they have learnt so far, to draft the content of a piece of writing. Once the content has been decided, pupils can concentrate on word and sentence level issues to complete their writing.

Overview

1 Select a significant moment from a text for discussion and analysis.
2 Introduce the concept of a freeze-frame as being similar to a pause on a video or an illustration in a book.
3 Invite individual pupils to represent the characters and use a label or simple item of costume to identify each character.
4 Taking each character in turn, ask the class where the character is likely to be looking and why. Demand evidence from the text to back up opinions; then select an appropriate direction for each character.
5 Make a draft freeze-frame to show the agreed positions of the characters.
6 Taking each character in turn, hold a cardboard thought-bubble over their heads and ask the class what the character might be thinking. Seek at least two alternative thoughts for each character and ask the pupil playing the character to select one from the suggestions.
7 Repeat the thought-bubble process with a heart-shaped card to indicate characters' feelings.
8 Make the freeze-frame and ask each character to voice their thoughts aloud. Alternatively invite other pupils to voice the characters' thoughts on their behalf, or agree each thought as a class and write the thoughts on blank cards for the class to read in chorus during the freeze-frame.
9 Invite some pupils to pass comments on each character from the readers' perspective. Then ask the class to identify aspects of the text that are responsible for giving the reader these perspectives. Ask what the author has written to influence pupils' interpretation of the text as expressed in the freeze-frame.

Year 7   Evacuees Write Home

A Literacy Lesson

Main focus: Developing inference and deduction, and writing in role

Link to specific text   *Goodnight Mr Tom* by Michelle Magorian

Links to the English Framework Objectives for Year 7

Drama:

S&L 15   develop drama techniques to explore in role a variety of situations and texts or respond to stimuli

S&L 18   develop drama techniques and strategies for anticipating, visualising and problem-solving in different learning contexts

Reading for meaning:

TLR 8   infer and deduce meanings using evidence in the text, identifying where and how meanings are implied

Understanding the author's craft:

TLR 14   recognise how writers' language choices can enhance meaning

TLR 16   distinguish between the attitudes and assumptions of characters and those of the author

Imagine, explore, entertain:

TLW 9   make links between their reading of fiction, plays and poetry and the choices they make as writers.

Preparation

1   Make sufficient copies of photocopiable sheets 1.1, 1.2 for all pupils and copies of photocopiable sheet 1.3 for less confident writers.

2   Draw a large thought-bubble on an A4 card. Write the word *THINKING* on it in large letters.

3   Draw a large heart shape on an A4 card. Write the word *FEELING* on it in large letters.

4   Write the word *READER* on an A4 card. Prepare adhesive name badges for the four characters in the freeze-frame, or collect one suitable prop or costume for each of them, such as: a luggage label on string for Willie; a green hat or silken scarf for the billeting officer; a waistcoat or woollen scarf for Tom and a teddy for the little girl.

5   Designate a small area in the room as a performance area, large enough for the four characters to stand in a line.

Introduction

1   Share the lesson objectives with the class and provide each pupil with a copy of photocopiable sheets 1.1 and 1.2.

2   Read the text to the class, whilst they follow the text on their copies of sheet 1.1. Then ask pupils to begin to fill in the response section on sheet 1.2, whilst you re-read the text to the class. After the two readings, allow pupils a few minutes to complete their sheets and then 1 minute to share their responses with a partner, before taking brief feedback.

3   Introduce the idea of making a freeze-frame to represent the quote underlined on the text. Select four pupils to represent the characters. Designate one end of the performance space as Tom's doorway and the other end as the iron gates. Position the characters with Tom and Willie by the door, and the billeting officer and the little girl near the gates. Then, invite the characters to put on their name badges, props or costumes.

4   Explain that the class will be expected to make the key decisions about the freeze-frame and *not* the character actors. Inform the class that this drama strategy is known as *forum theatre*.

Development

1   Invite Tom to stand in the doorway. Ask the class to consider where he is likely to be looking and

suggest that they give reasons for their responses, based on evidence in the text. If necessary, model the thinking by providing alternatives, for example:

Is Tom looking into the house because he has accepted the situation, or is he more likely to be looking at the billeting officer because he is still feeling angry and resentful?

2   Allow pupils between 1 and 2 minutes to scan the text, before you ask for responses. Make it clear that you will only consider versions that are backed up by evidence from the text. Pupils may have different versions, which will be equally valid. For example it could be argued that Tom is more likely to be looking at the billeting officer because it says in the text that 'He glared at Willie', which suggests that he is still feeling angry. Conversely it could be argued that he has accepted the situation, because his glaring was followed by the words 'You'd best come in', which implies that he is more likely to be looking into the house. Consider a few versions before allowing the pupil playing Tom to select a version from the ones suggested.

3   Repeat steps 1 and 2 for the other characters. The quote already indicates where Willie is looking, but prompt deeper responses for the other characters, for example:

Is the Billeting officer looking at Willie because she is concerned for his welfare, or is she more likely to be looking at the little girl because she has to get on with her job of finding homes for the other evacuees?

Encourage the pupils to scan the text for words to describe how the billeting officer is feeling, for example, 'harassed' and 'relieved'.

4   Explain that on the word *FREEZE*, the characters are to take up the agreed positions in the freeze-frame and hold the freeze whilst you say the words: *Willie watched her go . . . 1, 2, 3 . . . RELAX.* Now ask Tom to take up his freeze position again. Hold the thought-bubble above his head and ask the class to speculate on what he might be thinking, based on evidence from the text. Allow pupils a few minutes in pairs to write Tom's thoughts on a plain A4 sheet or on a white board. Include the pupils playing the characters in this task. Then ask some of the pupils to read out their suggestions. Select a thought based on textual evidence and give Tom the paper with the thought on. Repeat the above process with the other characters.

5   Re-create the freeze-frame, but this time ask the characters to speak their thoughts aloud in a given order. Alternatively, allocate four more pupils to stand behind the characters to read out their thoughts, or walk behind each character during the freeze-frame, allowing the class to read the thoughts chorally. Introduce this section by saying:

FREEZE . . . Willie watched her go . . . This is what they might have been thinking . . . (wait until the thoughts are spoken) *. . . 1, 2, 3 . . . RELAX.*

Some optional extension activities

1   Ask the characters to stand in a line in the performance area. To open up a discussion on how each character might be *feeling*, as opposed to *thinking,* hold the heart-shaped card over each character in turn to collect appropriate feelings. Hold the READER card above each character's head and ask the class the following 2 questions:

What do you, as readers, feel about this character?

What has the author written to make you feel the way you do about this character?

2   Challenge the class to change some of the author's words to see if they could alter the way a character is perceived by the reader, for example:

Change the words used to describe Mr Tom, so that he appears to be less threatening.

Writing in role

1   Ask the pupils to imagine that they were the other evacuees who witnessed the incident in the text. In pairs or threes, allow them a few minutes to discuss how they felt when they witnessed the incident and then take some feedback.

2   Explain that, by the end of the lesson each pupil will be asked to produce a draft copy of a letter sent home from an evacuee who witnessed the incident illustrated in the freeze-frame. To prepare for this, allow pupils 3 minutes to brainstorm some of the things they might say in their letters and then record these for them in note form on a flipchart or a white board. Now ask the pupils to share their ideas with a partner.

3   Ask individual pupils to use their ideas to plan and produce a draft letter within the next 10 to 15 minutes.

Differentiation
1   Allow less confident pupils to work in pairs using photocopiable sheet 1.3.
2   Encourage more confident pupils to invent extra information about the moment leading up to the incident and their own first night as an evacuee.

Plenary
1   Ask a few pupils to read out part of their draft letter and point out good practice.
2   Allow pairs of pupils a few minutes to identify between three and five important things that they can remember about the work in this lesson and then take brief feedback.
3   Lastly, link pupils' comments to the lesson objectives.

Year 7   Novel Moments

A Drama Lesson
Main focus: The novel – reflection and analysis
This session can be applied to any class novel, but it works best towards the end of the study of the novel.

Links to the English Framework Objectives for Year 7
Drama:
S&L 15   develop drama techniques to explore in role a variety of situations and texts or respond to stimuli
S&L 18   develop drama techniques and strategies for anticipating, visualising and problem-solving in different learning contexts.

Preparation
1   Write the lesson objectives onto a sheet of card so the class can read them from a distance.
2   Organise the pupils into mixed ability groups of four or five and create sufficient space for pupils to work practically in their groups.
3   Ensure each group has access to two copies of the text for reference and provide each group with a few sheets of white paper, a felt-tip pen and a piece of white A4 card.
4   Obtain a pack of large Post-Its and a fine felt-tip pen.

Introduction
1   Organise the pupils in a semi-circle around a clear space, which will be used as a performance area.
2   Share the lesson objectives with the class and link to the novel.
3   Provide pairs of pupils with a copy of the novel between them, then allow pupils a few minutes to suggest between one and three significant moments from the start of the novel, that would make a good opening scene if the novel were to be made into a video or film. Make it clear that they will be asked to justify their choices.
4   Select one of the suggested moments to re-create in a freeze-frame. Explain the concept of a freeze-frame as a video still, which puts the moment on hold.
5   Ask the class to suggest which characters would be in the freeze-frame and then select pupils to represent these characters. Write the characters' names on individual Post-Its and give them to each character to wear.
6   Explain that the class will make the key decisions about the freeze-frame, and not the actors. Inform the pupils that this strategy is known as *forum theatre*.
7   Ask the characters to stand in a line in the performance space. Discuss how they might be

arranged and go through each character in turn to discuss where they might be looking and what they might be feeling. If there is a disagreement, select one pupil to make the final decision or make it yourself based on what you feel is the most popular view. Discuss also how the actors might express a character's feelings in the way they position their bodies and the expressions on their faces.

8 Make a draft freeze-frame to see the effect so far. Ask the characters to hold the freeze to the count of 5. Explain that, in the final freeze-frame, the characters will be asked to speak an appropriate thought out loud. Taking each character in turn, ask for suggestions from the class to help the characters decide what to say. If a pupil playing a character is reluctant to speak their thought aloud, ask a more confident pupil to stand behind the character in the freeze-frame and speak that character's thought on their behalf.

9 Now make the final freeze-frame, but explain beforehand that the characters should freeze on the word *FREEZE* and then hold the freeze to the slow count of 5. Give the pupils 1 to 2 minutes to look through their copies of the novel to find an appropriate quote to accompany the freeze-frame. Take brief feedback.

Development

1 Organise the pupils into their groups of four or five and give them the following task:
   ● After 15 minutes, each group will be asked to present one or two freeze-frames with speaking thoughts.
   ● The freeze-frames should be based on one significant moment from the middle of the novel and one from towards the end.
   ● Each freeze-frame must be accompanied by an appropriate quote from the novel, which should be written on the cards provided.

2 Circulate among the groups to offer support. Encourage groups to think about how the characters might be feeling and how they could position the characters to make their freeze-frames look more interesting, for example, levels, groupings and positions.

3 Stop the activity after about 15 minutes, or when all groups have considered at least one freeze-frame. Give groups a few minutes to have a last rehearsal. Ask groups to decide who will read out their quote. Give groups the option to read their quote before, during or after the freeze-frame. Organise the pupils to sit in the semi-circle around the performance space and allow each group to present their freeze-frame with thoughts and a quote. Ask each group to explain their choice of moment and ask them to identify anything they would like to improve about the freeze-frame, if they were given more time. Then ask others to identify what they liked about the presentation.

Plenary

1 Remind the class of the lesson objectives and the three drama strategies they have used in the lesson i.e. freeze-frames, speaking thoughts/thought tracking and forum theatre.

2 Working in pairs, allow pupils a few minutes to identify between one and three important things that they can remember about the work in this lesson.

3 Take brief feedback, linking pupils' comments to the lesson objectives.

Year 8   Detecting the Bias

A Literacy Lesson
Main focus:
a) Introduction to the theme of the novel *Stone Cold* by Robert Swindells
b) Writing persuasive texts – exploring biased reporting in newspapers

Link to specific text *Stone Cold* by Robert Swindells

Links to the English Framework Objectives for Year 8

Drama:
S&L 14 develop the dramatic techniques that enable them to create and sustain a variety of roles
S&L 15 explore and develop ideas, issues and relationships through work in role
Reading for meaning:
TLR 6 recognise bias and objectivity, distinguishing facts from hypotheses, theories or opinions
Persuade, argue, advise:
TLW 13 present a case persuasively, making selective use of evidence, using appropriate rhetorical devices and anticipating responses and objections.

Preparation

1 Make sufficient copies of photocopiable sheets 1.4a, 1.4b and 1.5 for all pupils and copies of sheet 1.6 for less confident writers. Pairs of pupils will need one plain sheet of A4 paper or a white board.
2 Draw a large thought-bubble on an A4 card. Write the word *THINKING* on it in large letters.
3 Draw a large heart shape on an A4 card. Write the word *FEELING* on it in large letters.
4 Prepare adhesive name badges for *Shelter* and *Link*, and a sheet of paper saying *Homeless, please help*.
5 Obtain a coat or an old blanket as a prop (optional).
6 Designate a small area of the room as a performance area.

Introduction

1 Share the lesson objectives with the class.
2 Provide each pupil with a copy of the two extracts on photocopiable sheets 1.4a and 1.4b.
3 Read the texts to the class as an introduction to the novel *Stone Cold* by Robert Swindells.
4 Explain that you would like the class to assume that Link was the person who asked Shelter for money, and that you would like them to recreate the moment in a freeze-frame. If this is a new concept for the class, it can be compared to an illustration or a video still.
5 Select pupils to represent four characters: Link, a second homeless person, Shelter and another passer-by. Ask Link and Shelter to wear the name badges and introduce the sign and the coat or blanket as the only two props. If visibility could be a problem, allow the homeless to sit on chairs as if sitting on some steps.
6 Explain that it is the class who will be expected to make the key decisions about the freeze-frame, not the actors. Inform the class that this drama strategy is known as *forum theatre*.

Development

1 Ask the class to arrange the characters to depict Link and another homeless person asking Shelter and another passer by for money. Encourage them to refer to the texts for evidence of location, for example, Link is 'sitting in a doorway' and Shelter mentions that he 'marched along the Strand' and noticed the homeless 'dossing in all the doorways' just before he was asked for money.
2 Ask the class to refer to the text for clues on where the characters might be looking. For example, Link says that people avoid looking at him, so it's possible that the other passer-by would be looking away. Shelter, however, would be looking at Link, because he tells the reader that Link smiled at him.
3 Once the characters are positioned along with the props, place the thought-bubble beside each character in turn and ask the class to write down what that character might be thinking each time. Allow pupils a few minutes to discuss their ideas with a partner, before writing a thought on the A4 paper or white board in large letters. Encourage pupils to back up their ideas with evidence from the text where possible.
4 Ask the class to hold up their papers for everyone to see and/or select a few to discuss, before asking each actor to choose one of the thoughts for their character. Repeat this process with each character.

5   Explain that the actors should make the freeze-frame on the word *FREEZE*, and then speak out their thoughts in turn, as they hold the freeze. After the last character has spoken, they should wait until you say the words: *1, 2, 3 . . . RELAX.*

6   Now ask the actors to remain roughly in their positions, but they need not keep in freeze. Hold the heart-shaped card near each character in turn and ask the class what each character might be feeling. Give the class 30 seconds to think and then take ideas from volunteers. Link the responses back to the texts each time to ensure that responses are appropriate.

Writing as biased news reporters

1   Ask the class to imagine that the freeze-frame was a photograph that was published in the newspapers, on the day that the Government launched an inquiry into the problems of homeless people on the streets. It was published in three very different newspapers who reported the same incident in very different ways, according to their biased view. Use the following example to illustrate the bias of each paper.

2   Ask the class to imagine that one photographer from each paper went to a local open-air pop concert to take a photograph for their paper. Explain that the photographer from the paper called *The Governor* was asked to take a photograph showing how pop concerts cause problems with drink and drugs. However, there was no sign of any problems so he decided to take a photograph of the police compound. Explain that on the count of 3 the class are to stand up and make a freeze-frame of the police in this photograph. Talk about what they might be doing such as checking weapons, stroking police horses and dogs or putting on uniforms. When everyone has been given a minute to decide what they will be doing in the freeze, count to 3 and say the words:
FREEZE . . . This is the photograph that appeared in The Governor *and this is the headline:*
TROUBLE BREWING AT POP CONCERT – Police prepare!

3   Now move on to the photographer from *The People's Voice*. This photographer was asked to take a photograph of young people enjoying themselves without drugs and drink. There were a few people who were drunk but the photographer avoided them. This time ask the class to stand and represent a peaceful crowd enjoying their favourite band. Repeat the same process as before but this time the headline for the photograph in *The People's Voice* is:
YOUNG ENJOY MUSIC – and there's no hint of trouble.

4   Explain what happened to the third paper, *The City Independent*, without making a freeze-frame. Tell the class that this photographer wanted an accurate photograph showing a balanced view. So they took a random shot taking in both police and audience, and the headline was simply:
POP CONCERT GETS UNDERWAY WITH MINIMAL SIGNS OF TROUBLE.

5   Discuss the degree of bias inherent in each headline and link it to papers they may have read. Provide pairs with one copy of photocopiable sheet 1.5 and allow them a few minutes to complete the first task, involving allocating different headlines and captions to the appropriate papers.

6   Allocate one of the newspapers to every pair, but give the more confident writers *The City Independent* paper. Ask pupils to work in pairs as editors and allow them a few minutes to decide on a caption for the photograph, before taking suggestions. Point out good practice and explore ways to make the bias more pronounced, for example, using emotive words to describe the homeless such as the word 'dosser' used by Shelter. Collect positive and negative words or phrases to describe the homeless and record them on the board or on a flipchart for future reference. Then give pupils another minute to consider any changes they may now want to make to their captions to enhance or reduce the bias.

7   Now ask pairs to write the first draft of a short report to accompany their caption. Point out that the report must reflect the views of their paper as stated on photocopiable sheet 1.5. If necessary briefly discuss some of the techniques of persuasive writing, including the technique of identifying and then combating likely objections. Remind pupils that the focus of the report is about the homeless in general, rather than the characters, who may or may not be known to the press.

Differentiation

1   Support less confident pupils by putting them in role as editors, who make the final decisions about what articles should appear in their paper. Use photocopiable sheet 1.6 to provide the first few lines of the articles and ask them to complete the one that will appear under the photograph and caption in their particular newspaper.

2   In their role as editors for *The City Independent*, ask the more confident writers to provide a balanced viewpoint that acknowledges a range of perspectives on homelessness. Encourage them to support their arguments by inventing relevant comments made by the characters in the photograph and by allowing them to write a final version on completion of their draft.

Plenary

1   Ask some of the pupils to read out their draft reports and use this to point out good practice.
2   Link this biased writing to the biased perspective of Shelter in the text.
3   Working in pairs, allow pupils a few minutes to identify between three and five important things that they can remember about the work in this lesson. Then take some brief feedback, linking pupils' comments to the lesson objectives.

Year 8   Flashback

A Drama Lesson

Main focus: Exploring the flashback in Chapter 7 of *Holes*

Link to specific text   *Holes* by Louis Sachar

Links to the English Framework Objectives for Year 8

Drama:
S&L 14   develop the dramatic techniques that enable them to create and sustain a variety of roles
S&L 15   explore and develop ideas, issues and relationships through work in role.

Preparation

1   You will need a copy of *Holes* by Louis Sachar and/or copies of photocopiable sheet 1.7.
2   Pairs of pupils will need two sheets of paper and a pen between them.
3   Decide on a performance space and place a chair in the centre.

Introduction

1   Arrange the pupils in a semi-circle around the performance space. Ask the class to picture the scene as you read out an extract from *Holes* by Louis Sachar, pages 28–30. Read from the line 'Stanley's great-great-great grandfather was named Elya Yelnats' down to the line 'Against her better judgement, she agreed to help him'.
2   Explain that you would like the class to help two pupils create a freeze-frame of this moment. This can be compared to creating an illustration in the book or a video still. The moment should illustrate the line: 'Against her better judgement, she agreed to help him'.
    Select two pupils to represent Madame Zeroni and Elya and ask Madam Zeroni to sit in the chair in the performance space. Ask the class to decide where and how Elya should be positioned at the moment when Madame Zeroni agrees to help him, e.g. *Is he more likely to be standing, kneeling or sitting? Is he looking up at her or somewhere else?* Ask for reasons for each suggestion and then allow the character to make the final decision based on the suggestions made by the class.
3   When pupils are happy with the positioning of the two characters, ask the characters to make the freeze-frame by taking up a frozen position on the word *FREEZE*. Ask them to hold the freeze to the count of 5.
4   Explain that, in a few moments, the characters will be asked to repeat the freeze, but this time, members of the class will be asked to speak out the characters' thoughts.
5   Divide the class into two and allocate one half to Elya and the other half to Madame Zeroni. Allow pupils 1 to 2 minutes in pairs, to think of an appropriate thought for their character and decide which one of them will voice the thought and which one will point to the character as the thought is being voiced.

6 Repeat the freeze-frame, but this time ask the characters to hold the frozen position until all thoughts have been voiced. Allow pairs to take turns round the semi-circle to speak the thoughts and point to the character.

Development

1 Ask the characters to remain in the performance area, but allow them to relax their frozen positions. Take one of the pieces of plain A4 paper and ask the pupils what this might be, if there was some paper with writing on it somewhere in the freeze-frame. Make it clear that this paper could be on a wall, in someone's hand, or pocket or crumpled up on the floor. Take some suggestions, for example, a love letter from Elya to Myra that he never sent.

2 Then ask the pairs to take two pieces of paper and a pen between them and write something appropriate to include in the freeze-frame. They should write the same thing on both sheets, so that they can place one copy in the freeze-frame and retain the other. Give pupils a few minutes to complete this task and then ask them to take turns to place their papers in the freeze-frame. If a piece of writing is intended to go on a wall, place the paper on something that will represent the wall, such as a chair.

3 Ask the characters to make the freeze-frame again. Now move into the freeze-frame area and slowly pick up each piece of paper in turn. Start to read each paper aloud but let pairs of pupils finish off the readings using the copies they have retained. Make this a quiet and slow process to create a thoughtful atmosphere.

Optional group task

Ask pupils to predict how Madame Zeroni helped Elya. Then, working in pairs or threes, ask pupils to work out a short improvisation showing Elya telling one or two friends what happened when he went to see Madame Zeroni.

Plenary

1 Read the passage from *Holes* to the class and ask them to visualise the scene again, adding anything they have learned from this lesson. Read the blurb on the back of the novel and ask pupils to predict what this incident in the past might have to do with the boy in the detention camp.

2 Remind pupils of the three drama strategies employed in this lesson (freeze-frames, thought tracking and forum theatre) and make links with the lesson objectives.

Year 9   Macbeth's Banquet

A Literacy Lesson

Main focus: Analysis of The Banqueting Scene in *Macbeth* Act 3 Scene 4, lines 1–110

Link to specific text   *Macbeth* by William Shakespeare

Links to the English Framework Objectives for Year 9

Drama:

S&L 12   use a range of drama techniques, including work in role, to explore issues, ideas and meanings

S&L 13   develop and compare different interpretations of scenes or plays by Shakespeare or other dramatists

Study of literary texts:

TLR 14   analyse the language, form and dramatic impact of scenes and plays by published dramatists

Inform, explain, describe:

TLW 11   make telling use of descriptive detail e.g. *eye-witness accounts*.

Preparation

1 Pupils will need a copy of *Macbeth* Act 3 Scene 4, lines 1–110.
2 Make one copy of photocopiable sheets 1.8 and 1.9, for each pupil and copies of sheet 1.10 for pupils who would benefit from an extension task.
3 Draw a large thought-bubble on an A4 card. Write the word *THINKING* on it in large letters.
4 Draw a large heart shape on an A4 card. Write the word *FEELING* on it in large letters.
5 Write the lesson objectives where they can be seen by the whole class.
6 Arrange six spare chairs in a semi-circle at the front of the class.
7 Provide pairs of pupils with one sheet of plain A4 paper or a white board.

Introduction

1 Share the objectives with the class and inform them that by the end of the lesson they will have used three drama strategies (freeze-frames, thought tracking, forum theatre) to help them explore Shakespeare's ideas and meanings in *Macbeth* Act 3 Scene 4. Explain that you want the pupils to create a still image from Act 3 Scene 4, as if it were a pause or a freeze-frame on a video. The image will capture the moment just after Lady Macbeth has said the words 'You have displac'd the mirth, broke the good meeting, With most admir'd disorder'. Explain that creating a still image of this moment involves a dramatic technique known as a *freeze-frame*.
2 Give a copy of photocopiable sheet 1.8 to each pupil and copies of the text. Use the sheet to read the summary of the whole scene to the class and identify where the selected moment stands within the scene. Then ask confident readers to read Act 3 Scene 4, lines 1–110 aloud. Ask the rest of the class to try to imagine what the characters might be thinking and feeling as they follow the text on the sheet.
3 Inform the class that *they* will be asked to make the key decisions about the freeze-frame, rather than the pupils representing the characters. Explain that this strategy, known as *forum theatre*, will involve them in becoming directors.
4 Ask the pupils to decide which characters need to be in the freeze-frame. They should use evidence from the scene to make their decision. Explain that, due to limitations of space, only two pupils will be selected to represent the many Lords and Attendants.
5 Arrange six chairs at the front of the class. Select four pupils to play the parts of Macbeth, Lady Macbeth, Ross and Lennox. Then select two more pupils to represent the Lords and Attendants. Ask these pupils to sit on the chairs at the front of the class.

Development

1 Ask the class to consider where the actors should sit or stand and why. Encourage pupils to look in the text for clues about what Shakespeare envisaged and encourage them to consider the impact of the position of the characters on the audience, for example, *Who do we want the audience to focus on and why?* Emphasise that there could be a number of valid interpretations but a director can only select one. Examine the effect that each choice might have on the audience. Consider the implications of each suggestion for creating a particular atmosphere in the scene. If appropriate, link to the language and the positioning of this scene within the whole play to assess what atmosphere Shakespeare was trying to create. After discussion, select one interpretation from those suggested.
2 Taking each character in turn, ask the class to speculate on where that character is likely to be looking, based on the evidence in the text. Before accepting any responses, offer two alternatives, for example:
Is Lady Macbeth looking at Macbeth because she is thinking about how to stop him from behaving in this way, or is she more likely to be looking at the guests because she feels embarrassed?
These alternatives allow pupils inside the mind of the teacher to hear the thinking behind the analysis of a text. It may not have occurred to some pupils that there could be more than one perspective on a character's actions. This way of working encourages pupils to view a significant moment from the perspectives of the characters and emphasises the concept that literature is open to interpretation – providing it fits in with what we know of the text. Emphasise the fact that, as

directors, the class will need to consider several versions since each will have a different impact on the audience and affect the scene. If pupils are unable to agree on the final version, then you need to make the decision yourself, on the understanding that other versions are equally valid. On the word *FREEZE* ask the actors to take up their positions as agreed by the class. Ask them to hold their positions in freeze whilst you read out Lady Macbeth's final words (lines 109–110).

3 Then, ask the actors to remain roughly in position without being in freeze. Hold the thought-bubble over each of the character's heads in turn and ask the class to suggest what that character might be thinking, based on the text. Working in pairs, allow pupils a few minutes to write down an appropriate thought for each character on paper or on white boards. Take suggestions and allow the actors to select a thought for their character from these ideas. They should select one that they are prepared to speak out loud in the freeze-frame.

4 Ask the actors to make the freeze-frame again, but explain that this time they will be required to take turns to speak the thoughts out loud. Agree on the best order for the thoughts beforehand. Alternatively, choose other pupils to be the actors' voices. These pupils should stand behind the actors and speak out the characters' thoughts, either chorally or one voice per actor. Pupils playing the voices can be asked to speak the thoughts from memory or read out the thoughts from the white boards or papers.

5 Repeat the thought-bubble process with the heart shaped card to suggest characters' feelings as opposed to thoughts. To prepare for the forthcoming writing task, allow pupils a few minutes to work in pairs to discuss the feelings of the Lords and Attendants, before giving a response. If white boards are unavailable, pupils can use the reverse of the paper they used for the thought-bubbles. Ask the class or a group of pupils to put themselves in the role of the audience and ask them what they felt about each of the characters at the time of the freeze-frame. Then ask them to identify what language Shakespeare has used and how he has structured the events in order to make them feel the way they do about each character.

6 Ask all pupils to complete photocopiable sheet 1.9. Alternatively, (or as an extension task) ask each pupil to complete photocopiable sheet 1.10.

Plenary

1 Ask a few pupils to read out their written responses from photocopiable sheets 1.9 and 1.10 and use this to reinforce good practice.
2 Remind the pupils of the lesson objectives.
3 Working in pairs, allow pupils a few minutes to identify between one and three important things that they can remember about the work in this lesson.
4 Link pupils' comments to the lesson objectives.

Year 9   Macbeth meets the Witches

A Literacy Lesson
Main focus: Analysis of *Macbeth* Act 4 Scene 1

Link to specific text   *Macbeth* by William Shakespeare

Links to the English Framework Objectives for Year 9
Drama:
S&L 13   develop and compare different interpretations of scenes or plays by Shakespeare or other dramatists

Preparation

1 Write the lesson objective where all the class can see it.
2 Ensure every pupil has access to a copy of *Macbeth* Act 4 Scene 1, and some rough paper and a pen.
3 Draw a large thought-bubble on an A4 card. Write the word *THINKING* on it in large letters.
4 Make one copy of each of photocopiable sheets 1.11 and 1.12 and place them in individual plastic wallets.
5 Organise pupils into pairs and ensure there is enough space for a group of up to 10 pupils to stand in a performance area.

Introduction

1 Share the lesson objective with the class.
2 Arrange the pupils in a semi-circle around the performance area.
3 Provide pupils with copies of the text and if necessary summarise the main events before reading the text aloud to the class. Read the part of Macbeth yourself and select the most confident readers to read the other parts.
4 Now re-read lines 66–75, which cover the appearance of the first apparition. Explain that you would like the class to help one group of pupils to create a freeze-frame of the moment after the first apparition has spoken the lines:
   'Macbeth, Macbeth, Macbeth: beware Macduff, Beware the Thane of Fife. Dismiss me. Enough.'
   Discuss the general meaning of these lines to ensure the class understand the message that Macbeth has just received.
5 Select three pupils to represent the witches, one pupil to represent Macbeth and one pupil to hold Card 1 representing the first apparition. Discuss where the characters might best be positioned in terms of staging the scene. Refer to the text to check that suggestions are viable before making any decisions. If the class are not able to agree on the positions of the characters, then make a decision yourself based on what you feel are the most popular and credible suggestions. Point out that there could be, and have been, several interpretations of this scene, but only one can be selected here for the purposes of the freeze-frame.
6 Make a practice freeze-frame by asking the characters to take up their agreed positions when you say the word *FREEZE*. Explain that the characters should maintain the freeze, whilst one of the pupils reads lines 69–71 aloud from Card 2. The actors should continue to hold the freeze until you say: *1, 2, 3 . . . RELAX*.

Development

1 Explain that in the final freeze-frame, the actors will be given voices to speak their character's thoughts out loud. The *voices* will stand behind the characters in the freeze-frame. However, make it clear that you will be using a drama strategy known as *forum theatre*, where the class will be responsible for deciding the thoughts.
2 Explain the need to identify what Macbeth said immediately after hearing the apparition, in order to decide what he could be thinking. Refer to lines 72–73 and help the class to summarise Macbeth's response to the first apparition. Record a simple version of this response, in modern language on the board, for example: *Thankyou for your warning. You have told me what I was already fearful of . . .*
3 Now ask the actors to make the practice freeze-frame again as before, but this time ask the class to consider what Macbeth might be thinking. As the actors make the freeze-frame, ask a pupil to hold the thought-bubble over Macbeth's head.
4 Working in pairs, allow the pupils 1 to 2 minutes to write down one suggestion for the contents of Macbeth's thought-bubble. Then take some suggestions and nominate a pupil to be Macbeth's voice. Invite this pupil to select a thought from all the ideas.
5 Without making the practice freeze-frame again, hold the thought-bubble over the heads of the witches and discuss what they might be thinking, as a group of three. Then nominate a pupil to represent the voice of the witches. After discussion, ask the class to suggest an appropriate thought

and invite the pupils representing the voice of the witches to make the final decision. Record the thought on paper and give it to the *voice*.

6 Ask the pupils playing the *voices* to stand behind their characters, in preparation for the final freeze-frame. Explain beforehand that the *voices* should stand upright in a neutral position, whilst the actors make the freeze. The actors should hold the freeze whilst you read the lines on Card 2 and then the *voices* should read out their thoughts in a pre-arranged order.

7 Repeat the above process for the appearance of the second and then the third apparition, using the lines on the appropriate cards. Alternatively, ask pupils to work in groups to prepare their own versions.

Plenary

Link the work to the lesson objective and remind pupils of the three drama strategies employed in this lesson (freeze-frames, thought tracking and forum theatre).

UNIT TWO   SYMBOLIC BODY SCULPTURES

Making Links

Links to the National Curriculum Key Stages 3 and 4 English Programmes of Study

Drama: **S&L 4**   To participate in a range of drama activities and to evaluate their own and others' contributions, pupils should be taught to use a variety of dramatic techniques to explore ideas, issues, texts and meanings.

Links to the English Framework Objectives

Year 7
Drama: **S&L 15, 18**
Reading for meaning: **TLR 7**
Plan, draft and present: **TLW 1**

Year 8
Drama: **S&L 15**
Reading for meaning: **TLR 5**
Plan, draft and present: **TLW 1**

Year 9
Drama: **S&L 12**
Study of literary texts: **TLR 14, 18**
Plan, draft and present: **TLW 2**
Vocabulary: **Wd 7**

Links to Schemes of Work

Narrative poetry / ballads; Poetry, novels and plays concerned with issues

Links to specific texts

Year 7   *The Pied Piper of Hamelin* by Robert Browning

Year 8   *Digging* by Seamus Heaney; *My Hero* by Willis Hall; *Lullaby* by Rosemary Norman; *Catrin* by Gillian Clarke; *Poem* by Simon Armitage

Year 9   Extracts from *Macbeth; Twelfth Night;* and *A Midsummer Night's Dream* by William Shakespeare; *The Outsiders* by S.E. Hinton

Definitions

Symbolic body sculpture is produced by positioning a group of pupils in such as way as to represent a sculpture, which symbolises a theme, issue or storyline. Sculptures can have titles such as *Bullying, Love and Hate, Dickensian London* or *The Story of the Pied Piper*. Sometimes a key object is incorporated into the sculpture, such as a pipe for the Pied Piper. The pupils in the sculpture are usually placed in particular positions according to the decisions made by other pupils. There are several ways of organising this technique, but the simplest way is for the teacher to guide the class in creating a sculpture using just a small group of pupils at the front of the class.

Teaching and Learning Rationale

The need to represent something abstract or multifaceted in a single physical statement such as a sculpture, works to promote discussion on a symbolic level. For example, if Year 9 pupils were asked to create a sculpture based on the theme of power and/or ambition in *Macbeth*, they could be encouraged to consider a range of images representing the different facets of power and ambition in Shakespeare's play.

This activity encourages pupils to engage with texts, ideas and issues on a deeper, more meaningful level and caters for pupils who prefer to learn through visual and kinaesthetic teaching methods.

The work can also be productively linked to writing, by asking pupils to present a concise summary of their thinking in the form of an inscription for the sculpture.

Overview

1   Select a theme, issue or text that could be explored through symbolic sculpture and provide copies of the text.
2   Select approximately six pupils who will represent the sculpture, and any key objects that are to be included. Then create a small performance space.
3   Fold a piece of A4 card so that it stands up. Select an appropriate title for the sculpture and write this on the card in large letters. The title could be the title of a story or poem, a quote from a text, or a description of an issue such as *Gender Stereotypes* or *Faces of Friendship*. Refer to the title on the card and ask the class to imagine that a sculpture with this title was exhibited in a public place.
4   Explain that the class will be responsible for creating the imaginary sculpture, using the pupils at the front and any key objects if appropriate. Spend some time discussing how the pupils and objects could be arranged, to make the sculpture represent the title.
5   Then arrange the pupils according to the most popular ideas and ask them to remain in a frozen position to give the illusion of a sculpture. They should hold this position to the count of 5, whilst the class view the final effect. If necessary discuss any minor adjustments and then make the sculpture again.
6   Work with the whole class to begin to compose an inscription for the sculpture. This should elaborate on the theme or story and complement the title. Then ask pupils to complete the inscription, working on their own.

Year 7   The Pied Piper

A Literacy Lesson

Main focus:
a) Analysis of relationships and issues in the poem *The Pied Piper of Hamelin*
b) Writing concise summaries

Link to specific text   *The Pied Piper of Hamelin* by Robert Browning

Links to the English Framework Objectives for Year 7

Drama:

S&L 15   develop drama techniques to explore in role a variety of situations and texts or respond to stimuli

S&L 18   develop drama techniques and strategies for anticipating, visualising and problem-solving in different learning contexts

Reading for meaning:

TLR 7   identify the main points, processes or ideas in a text and how they are sequenced and developed by the writer

Plan, draft and present:

TLW 1   plan, draft, edit, revise, proofread and present a text with readers and purpose in mind.

Preparation

1 Note that all pupils need to be familiar with the storyline of the narrative poem *The Pied Piper* and should have read at least some of the original text prior to this lesson.
2 Select a group of six or seven pupils who will form the sculpture and create a small space at the front of the class with room for the sculpture group to sit in or near the space.
3 Obtain a copy of the poem for each pupil, and a recorder or an object such as a ruler, to represent the Pied Piper's pipe.
4 Write an adhesive name badge or obtain a prop or costume such as a gold chain or a cloak to represent the mayor.
5 Fold a piece of A4 card so that it stands up. Write the words: *The Story of the Pied Piper of Hamelin* on the card in large letters.
6 Obtain the use of a camera (optional).
7 Make sufficient copies of the differentiated photocopiable sheets 2.1 and 2.2 for the pupils, as required.

Introduction

1 Share the lesson objectives with the class.
2 Link to prior learning through the following activity: organise the class into pairs or threes and allow them a few minutes to recall between three and five important facts about the story of the Pied Piper. Then select pairs to share a few facts, until the basic story has been covered.
3 Invite the pupils who will become the symbolic body sculpture to sit in or near the designated space.
4 Ask the class to imagine that the people in the modern village of Hamelin want to create a sculpture to commemorate, or remind people of the story of the Pied Piper. Introduce the card with the title of the sculpture written on it. Explain that the class' challenge will be to create a suitable idea for a sculpture, using the selected pupils as their imaginary clay. Explain also that the sculpture can include the pipe and mayor's items if they wish.

Development

1 Spend some time discussing which characters would be in the sculpture, and how they would be positioned. Use individuals or pairs of pupils to represent large groups such as the children, the townspeople, the parents and the rats. Alternatively, use objects such as rolled up jumpers to represent the rats if pupils find it difficult to represent them. Extend pupils' thinking by asking them to consider certain questions before they make their final decisions on the sculpture.

Here are some possible questions:

Who should be in the sculpture and why?
Should the person or people who are to blame for the loss of the children have a central position?
Is one person to blame or should everyone share some of the blame?
Will the sculpture be biased in favour of our own views or should it attempt to be impartial?
Who does the poet think is to blame? Does the poem give us any clues?

2 Encourage frequent reference to the poem for evidence to back up any decisions. Eventually, base the sculpture on the most popular decisions and instruct the pupils at the front to make the sculpture accordingly. Ask them to hold their positions to the count of 5, so that the class can assess the effect. If any minor alterations are necessary, make the sculpture again with the revisions.
3 Taking a photograph of the sculpture can raise the status of the activity, assist follow up work and serve to complement a display of written work. It can also be a useful means of providing evidence of drama should this be required (optional).
4 Suggest that you work with the class to write an inscription to accompany the title of the sculpture. Explain that inscriptions have to be written in a limited space. Mention the fact that readers of such inscriptions are often just passing by and would not want to read a long passage. Give a word count of around 50–75 words and work with the class to compose a rough draft of the inscription.

Model writing the first few lines before involving the class. Issues of bias and the need to attract the casual reader should be introduced to pupils if these do not arise naturally.

5   Organise the class into pairs of similar ability. Give confident pupils a copy of photocopiable sheet 2.1 and those needing more support a copy of sheet 2.2. Allow all pairs to discuss their ideas before completing their sheets.

Plenary

1   Select a few pairs to feedback on their inscriptions and point out examples of good practice. Ask the class to identify why you consider these examples to be good practice.
2   Remind the pupils of the lesson objectives.
3   Give the pairs of pupils a few minutes to identify between one and three important things that they can remember about the work in this lesson. Then take brief feedback.
4   Finally, lead the discussion to help pupils assess how far they have succeeded in achieving the stated objectives and if appropriate identify what they need to do next. This provides an opportunity to reinforce the main points that have arisen from the sculpture and the written work.

Year 8   Family Relationships

A Literacy Lesson

Main focus: An introduction to poems presenting a range of perspectives on family relationships

Links to specific texts   *Digging* by Seamus Heaney; *My Hero* by Willis Hall; *Lullaby* by Rosemary Norman; *Catrin* by Gillian Clarke; *Poem* by Simon Armitage

Links to the English Framework Objectives for Year 8
Drama:
S&L 15   explore and develop ideas, issues and relationships through work in role
Reading for meaning:
TLR 5   trace the development of themes, values or ideas in texts
Plan, draft and present:
TLW 1   experiment with different approaches to planning, drafting, proofreading and presenting writing, taking account of the time available.

Preparation

1   Ensure all pupils have access to copies of the poems on photocopiable sheets 2.3a, 2.3b, 2.4a and 2.4b and access to a few sheets of plain paper and pencils.
2   You will need access to a white board or flipchart.
3   Select a group of 6 or 7 pupils who will form the sculpture, and create a performance space with sufficient room for the sculpture group to stand in formation.
4   Obtain a pad of adhesive name badges or Post-It notes, and a felt-tip pen (optional).
5   Obtain an item to represent a baby in a shawl, for example, a jumper or small blanket.
6   Fold a piece of A4 card so that it stands up. Write the words *Family Relationships* on the card in large letters.

Introduction

1   Share the lesson objectives with the class, and explain how this lesson will serve as an introduction to poetry on the theme of Family Relationships.
2   Position the card saying *Family Relationships* in the performance space and explain that the class will be asked to create an imaginary sculpture of this title, using six or seven people. Ask the pupils who will form the sculpture to stand or sit near the performance space.

3 Explain that the class will be asked to make a sculpture of the stereotypical family as presented in the media. Ask the class to decide on what members of a family make up the stereotype. This is likely to be a nuclear family or an extended family, but the final decision should be the pupils'. Allocate pupils to family members, using the adhesive name badges if appropriate. Use the item of clothing if you need to represent a baby.

4 Give pupils a few minutes in pairs, to discuss how the family members could be arranged to represent ideal family relationships as depicted in the media. Pupils should discuss where each family member should stand in relation to the others and how they would be positioned. Pupils should also discuss appropriate facial expressions to reflect the feelings of family members in the sculpture.

5 Take feedback, asking some of the pairs to demonstrate their suggestions by directing the sculpture group into the desired effect. Make it clear that the final decision for the sculpture lies with the majority of the class, but in the absence of a clear majority, you will make the final decision based on their ideas.

6 Finally, ask the six or seven pupils to make the agreed sculpture and hold it to a count of 5, so the class can consider the image. Quickly make a rough sketch of the sculpture on the board, using stick people. Explain that the rough sketch will be useful when the class have to re-create the sculpture later in the lesson. It also serves as a model for using sketching as an approach to planning a piece of writing.

Development

1 Help the class to explore two relatively positive views of family relationships, by introducing them to the poems *Digging* by Seamus Heaney and *My Hero* by Willis Hall (see photocopiable sheets 2.3a and 2.3b). As an introduction, it is best to focus on the meanings of the poems at this stage, rather than a full analysis. Follow this by exploring the meanings of one or two other poems which have a different perspective on family relationships, such as: *Lullaby* by Rosemary Norman; *Catrin* by Gillian Clarke and *Poem* by Simon Armitage (see photocopiable sheets 2.4a and 2.4b).

2 Now ask the sculpture group to reform their original sculpture for a moment to remind the class of the ideal image of family relationships. Working in pairs, allow pupils between 2 and 3 minutes to discuss how they might adapt their original sculpture to reflect both the positive and negative images of family relationships presented in the poems. Make it clear that this second sculpture will be a representation of the images presented in the poems, and therefore may not necessarily reflect their own image of family relationships. Invite pupils to use sketches to develop their ideas if they wish.

3 Take feedback through practical demonstration as before, and use this as a means to discuss the issues in the poems in more depth. Decide on a final sculpture and ask the pupils originally selected to create the revised version.

4 Allow pupils between 3 and 5 minutes to make some draft sketches of a sculpture of *Family Relationships*, to reflect their own views. Before the pupils begin this task, explain that making sketches can be used to explore and develop ideas for writing. Inform the pupils that they will eventually use their sketches to help them draft their own poems on the theme of *Family Relationships*. Make it clear that, since the sketches are for planning purposes only, the quality of the drawing is not important, although the meaning must be clear. Pupils should make very quick, rough sketches using stick people similar to your previous sketch on the board.

5 When most pupils have attempted a sketch, allow pupils a few minutes to explain their sketches to a partner. Ask pupils to use the ideas contained in their sketches to help them draft their own individual poems linked to the theme of *Family Relationships*.

Plenary

1 Ask some pupils to read out parts of their draft work and use this to reinforce good practice.
2 Remind the pupils of the lesson objectives.
3 Allow pairs of pupils a few minutes to identify between one and three important things they can remember about the work of this lesson.
4 Take brief feedback, linking the pupils' comments to the lesson objectives.
5 The draft poems can be completed in a subsequent lesson or for homework.

Year 8   Family Drama

A Drama Lesson

Main Focus: Exploring family issues and relationships

 Links to specific texts: *Digging* by Seamus Heaney; *My Hero* by Willis Hall; *Lullaby* by Rosemary Norman; *Catrin* by Gillian Clarke; *Poem* by Simon Armitage

Links to the English Framework Objectives for Year 8

Drama:

S&L 15   explore and develop ideas, issues and relationships through work in role

Reading for meaning:

TLR 5   trace the development of themes, values or ideas in texts.

Preparation

1   Ensure all pupils have access to copies of *My Hero* and *Poem* and/or *Lullaby* (see photocopiable sheets 2.3b, 2.4a and 2.4b).
2   Ensure sufficient space for pupils to work practically in small groups and then organise pupils into groups of about four to five pupils.
3   Use pupils' jumpers or obtain some small pieces of material to represent babies in shawls.

Introduction

1   Share the lesson objectives with the class and begin as in the Introduction to the Year 8 literacy lesson on p. 18, by creating a small group sculpture on the stereotypical media version of the theme of *Family Relationships*.

Development

Omit the remainder of the Year 8 literacy lesson and conduct the drama lesson as follows:

1   Read and discuss the meanings of the two or three selected poems.
2   Organise the class into groups of four to five pupils.
3   Ask some groups to create and present a symbolic body sculpture entitled *My Hero*, using some of the images from this poem. Ask other groups to do the same with *Poem* and/or *Lullaby*. Give pupils a time limit of around 10 minutes for this work, and make it clear that each group will be expected to explain their sculpture to the rest of the class.

Plenary

1   Discuss and/or ask each group to prepare and present a symbolic body sculpture, which reflects a balanced view of modern family life in Britain.
2   Remind the class of the lesson objectives and discuss how they link to this work.
3   Use this lesson as an introduction to a unit of work based on other poems on this theme.

Year 9   Shakespeare's Language

A Literacy Lesson Starter Activity

Main focus: Language in Shakespeare – understanding and appreciating metaphors

This activity works best when pupils have some initial working knowledge of the chosen play.

Links to specific texts   *Macbeth; Twelfth Night;* and *A Midsummer Night's Dream* by William Shakespeare

Links to the English Framework Objectives for Year 9

Drama:

S&L 12   use a range of drama techniques, including work in role, to explore issues, ideas and meanings

Study of literary texts:

TLR 14   analyse the language, form and dramatic impact of scenes and plays by published dramatists

Vocabulary:

Wd 7   recognise layers of meaning in the writer's choice of words.

Preparation

1   Select one or two metaphors or phrases from a Shakespearian play that lend themselves to imagery, for example:

Macbeth: (Act 1 Scene 5, lines 62–63) LADY MACBETH 'look like th'innocent flower, / But be the serpent under't.'

(Act 1 Scene 7, lines 25–28) MACBETH 'I have no spur / To prick the sides of my intent, but only / Vaulting ambition, which o'er-leaps itself, / And falls on th'other.'

Twelfth Night: (Act 1 Scene 1, lines 1–3) DUKE ORSINO 'If music be the food of love, play on, / Give me excess of it, that, surfeiting, / The appetite may sicken, and so die.'

A Midsummer Night's Dream: (Act 2 Scene 1, line 175) PUCK 'I'll put a girdle round about the earth / In forty minutes.'

2   Write your selected quotation on an A4 card and fold the card so it will stand up.

3   Create a small performance space large enough for four or five pupils to stand in a group formation.

4   Select groups of 4 or 5 pupils to represent each metaphor.

5   Obtain the use of a camera (optional).

Introduction

1   Read the quotation to the class and ask them to guess the exact context, or its approximate position in the sequence of events in the play.

2   Explain that this starter activity will help the class understand and recall the quotation and its context.

Development

1   Place the quotation card over the back of a chair or on a table, close to the performance area.

2   Ask the class to imagine that this quotation is the title of a sculpture in a gallery. Explain that the class will be asked to create this sculpture by positioning four or five pupils as if they were clay figures.

3   Ask the group who will represent the sculpture to move into or near the performance space.

4   Give pupils a few minutes in pairs, to think of suggestions on what the sculpture would look like and why. Pupils should discuss positions and include facial expressions if appropriate. If pupils find the concept difficult, then make a couple of suggestions yourself, for example, 'If music be the food of love . . .' could be represented by one pupil playing an instrument, whilst another indicates they are eating a meal. The rest of the quotation would need to link with an image of love and illustrate how surfeit dulls the appetite so that love is rejected.

5   Now ask pupils to direct the sculpture group according to their ideas, so the class can consider the effect. Make it clear that the decision for the sculpture lies with the majority view of the class. However, if the class cannot agree, then you will need to make the decision based on their ideas.

6   Ask the sculpture group to position themselves into the final sculpture. They should hold the position as the class read the quotation aloud.

7   Take a photograph of the sculpture and display it with the quotation (optional).

Year 9   The Outsiders

A Drama Lesson

Main focus: Introduction to the novel *The Outsiders*

Link to specific text   *The Outsiders* by S.E. Hinton

Links to the English Framework Objectives for Year 9

Drama:

S&L 12   use a range of drama techniques, including work in role, to explore issues, ideas and meanings

Study of literary texts:

TLR 18   discuss a substantial prose text, sharing perceptions, negotiating common readings and accounting for differences of view.

Preparation

1   Ensure sufficient space for pupils to work practically, in small groups and identify a performance area near to a board or flipchart.
2   The class will need to work in pairs, who will then join up to form groups of four.
3   Take one copy of the novel into the lesson, but keep it hidden until the plenary.
4   Fold an A4 card so that it stands up and write the words *Friends and Outsiders* on it in large letters.

Introduction

1   Share the objectives with the class and explain that the work will serve as an introduction to a novel which you will reveal in the plenary.
2   Arrange the class to sit in a semi-circle around the performance area.
3   Place the *Friends and Outsiders* card in a central position in the performance area. Ask the class to imagine that this is the title of a sculpture, made up of a number of clay figures. Explain that this lesson will involve the class making this sculpture using their own bodies to represent the clay figures.
4   Organise the class to work in pairs. Ask one pupil in each pair to name themselves as **A** and the other as **B**. If numbers are odd, allow a group of three to work as two **As** and a **B**.
5   Ask all the **A** pupils to stand in a large circle facing inwards. Now ask the **Bs** to face their partners to make an inner circle (see diagram for example).

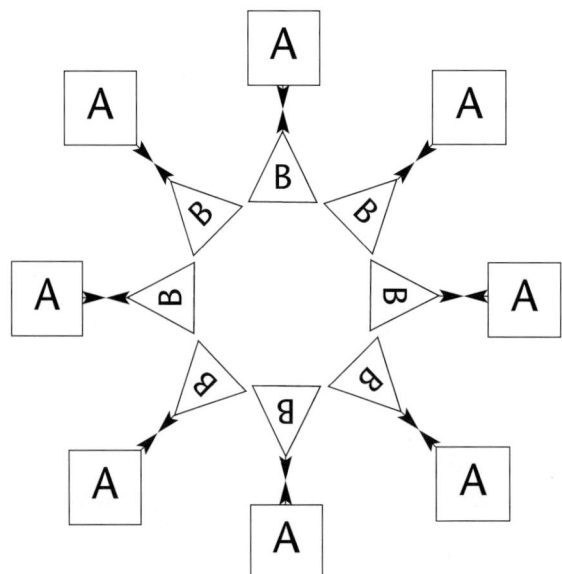

6 Discuss a range of possible images to represent the part of the sculpture that symbolises *Friends*. This could include abstract images to represent qualities such as kindness and trust, or realistic incidents such as sharing food or talking on the phone.

7 Working in pairs where they are standing, ask each of the **A** pupils (or pairs of **As**) to select an image of friendship and then sculpt their partner **B** into that image. Explain that the idea is to make the inner circle of **B** pupils into a corporate sculpture representing the *Friends* part of the title. Make it clear that the **As** are to *demonstrate* and *explain* to their partners how they wish them to be positioned, rather than physically moving them. Ask the **As** to step back from the inner circle when they have finished their sculpting. Give the class a completion time of 1 minute from when the first **As** finish.

8 Ask the **Bs** to remain in position, whilst the **A** pupils walk around the sculpture to view the different images of friendship. Make it clear that the **A** pupils may comment on the sculpture, but they are not to communicate with or make personal comments about the pupils in the sculpture. Make this fairly brisk to avoid the **B** pupils having to keep still for an unacceptable length of time.

9 Allow **As** and **Bs** to change places and repeat the process to make a symbolic sculpture containing images of *Outsiders*. Use the work to encourage full discussion on the concept of an outsider.

Development

1 Organise the pupils to sit as an audience. Then invite three pairs at a time to take up their sculptured positions. Each pair should present their images opposite each other, to form three smaller sculptures of *Friends and Outsiders*. Ask each pair to explain their choice of image and invite constructive comments from the rest of the class.

2 Invite the class to create a written definition of the terms *Friends* and *Outsiders* to accompany the sculpture, and write these on a white board or flipchart.

3 Let each pair join with another pair, to devise and present a short 1 to 2 minute improvisation of a conversation between three friends and an outsider who tries to join the group. Make it clear that this should involve dialogue only and should not include any offensive language.

Differentiation

Ask more confident groups to produce an improvisation with two different outcomes: one where the outsider is accepted into the group and another where the outsider is rejected. Invite groups to present their improvisations to the rest of the class. Use this as an opportunity to deepen pupils' understanding of the concept of outsiders and to reinforce good performance skills.

Plenary

1 Reveal the novel *The Outsiders* to the class, and read aloud the first few pages down to the line 'I'm not saying that either Socs or Greasers are better; that's just the way things are.' As they listen to the extract, ask them to make connections between what they hear and what they have discussed in this lesson.

2 After reading the passage, allow pairs 1 or 2 minutes to discuss these connections before taking brief feedback.

3 Link pupils' comments to the lesson objectives.

UNIT THREE   CONSCIENCE ALLEY

Making Links

Links to the National Curriculum Key Stages 3 and 4 English Programmes of Study

Drama: **S&L 4**   To participate in a range of drama activities and to evaluate their own and others' contributions, pupils should be taught to use a variety of dramatic techniques to explore ideas, issues, texts and meanings.

Links to the English Framework Objectives

Year 7
Drama: **S&L 15, 18**
Persuade, argue, advise: **TLW 15**
Stylistic conventions of non-fiction: **Sn 13f**
Speaking: **S&L 5**

Year 8
Drama: **S&L 15**
Analyse, review, comment: **TLW 16**
Group discussion and interaction: **S&L 10**

Year 9
Drama: **S&L 12**
Analyse, review, comment: **TLW 16**
Speaking: **S&L 2**
Group discussion and interaction: **S&L 9**

Links to Schemes of Work

Discursive writing

Definition

Conscience Alley is produced by someone in role as a character, walking round the classroom towards a dilemma written on a card. As the character walks past the pupils, they put forward contrasting points of view to help the character solve the dilemma. The character's route or alleyway can be made up of pupils standing opposite each other in two lines or it can be a pathway cleared through desks.

In preparation for the strategy, points for and against a course of action are recorded on two separate sheets of paper on opposite sides of the room. Pupils order the points so that they are linked together as arguments and counter-arguments. Pupils can use the points on the sheets to draft and write a balanced discursive argument.

Teaching and Learning Rationale

The strength of this strategy lies in the way it helps pupils learn to present a *balanced* argument through visual and kinaesthetic teaching methods. Opposing points of an argument are physically represented and separated, as pupils take an active part in the strategy. Conscience Alley can be used successfully to improve pupils' speaking and listening skills during a drama lesson, or adapted to help pupils think, communicate and write balanced accounts of issues or dilemmas in a literacy lesson. It can also be used successfully alongside texts such as *The Discussion Book* by Sue Palmer (TTS Group) or *New Hodder English 3* (Unit 5, p. 112, Both Sides Of The Argument) by Sue Hackman, Alan Howe and Patrick Scott (Hodder & Stoughton *Educational*).

Overview

1 Select an issue or dilemma that lends itself to two diametrically opposed points of view, for example:
   Should zoos be banned? or *Should archaeologists be allowed to take something from the dig for themselves?*

2 Select a role or character who would need to make a choice between the two points of view, for example: a planning officer who has a request for a zoo in the town, or Howard Carter considering whether to take something from the tomb of Tutankhamen.

3 Write a name card or select an object to represent the issue, for example: a picture of a zoo animal to represent a zoo or a golden ornament to represent the treasures of Tutankhamen. Place this card or object on a chair at the back of the room.

4 Place two large sheets of paper on the wall, one at either side of the room, near the front of the class. Use a different colour pen for each sheet. Write the word *For* on one sheet and *Against* on the other and fill in what they relate to, for example: **For** allowing the zoo to be built and **Against** allowing the zoo to be built.

5 Clear a route from the front of the class to the card or object on the chair. The route should enable the role to pass as many pupils as possible.

6 Organise pupils into pairs, and allow them a few minutes to record between three and five things they know about the selected issue or dilemma. Then take feedback.

7 Introduce the role and explain that the class will represent the role's thoughts, as he or she grapples with points for and against the stated course of action.

8 Explain that pupils sitting in the half of the room nearest the *For* sheet will represent the points on the *For* sheet and the other half will represent the points on the *Against* sheet.

9 Allow pairs a few minutes to record between one and three points for their sheet i.e. for their given side of the argument. Then take ideas and record these on the sheets of paper. Record each of these in the form of a list of short sentences written in the first person, as if they were the character's thoughts. Link arguments to counter arguments as they are discussed.

10 Allocate each pair one sentence from their designated sheet. Some will have the same sentence as another if there are more pairs than sentences.

11 Take on the role and walk along the route. Ask pupils to read out their sentences as you pass them by. Explain beforehand that when you reach the card or object on the chair, the pupils should quietly call out their sentences simultaneously, to create the effect of contrasting thoughts going round in the person's mind. Say *FREEZE* to stop the exercise.

12 Ask pupils to compose a discursive piece of writing on the issue. Allow pupils to refer to the points on the sheets and use a supporting text such as *The Discussion Book* by Sue Palmer to help them.

Year 7   Should We Ban Zoos?

A Literacy Lesson

Main focus: Writing a discursive essay on the issue of zoos

 Links to the English Framework Objectives for Year 7

Drama:

S&L 15 develop drama techniques to explore in role a variety of situations and texts or respond to stimuli

S&L 18 develop drama techniques and strategies for anticipating, visualising and problem-solving in different learning contexts

Persuade, argue, advise:
TLW 15 express a personal view, adding persuasive emphasis to key points
Stylistic conventions of non-fiction:
Sn 13 f) *Discursive writing* which signposts the organisation of contrasting points and clarifies the
      viewpoint.

Preparation

1 Fold a piece of A4 card so that it can stand up, and write the words: *I will vote to keep the zoo*
    on the card in large letters.
2 Organise pupils into pairs, who will sit together at the same desk, and ensure they have a supply of
    rough paper and pencils.
3 Plan a route around the classroom that will ensure you pass as many pairs of pupils as possible.
    Place an empty chair or a table at the end of the route.
4 Place a large sheet of paper on the wall at one side of the room and write the words *For keeping
    the zoo* at the top in large letters. Then place another paper on the other side of the room and write
    Against keeping the zoo on it, using a different coloured pen.
5 Write a list of suitable phrases and connectives on the blackboard, that could be used to link
    arguments in a discursive essay, for example: *however, it could argued that, alternatively.*
6 Make one copy of photocopiable sheet 3.1, and cut out the points in strips.

Introduction

1 Share the lesson objectives with the class.
2 Access prior learning by allowing pairs of pupils a few minutes to write down what they associate
    with the word *zoo* and then take very brief feedback.
3 Give out the strips of paper (one per pair) from photocopiable sheet 3.1. In large classes, some
    pairs will not have a strip, so make it clear that everyone is expected to contribute to the
    discussion. Ask the pair with strip **1+** to read out their point and then ask if another pair has a
    point that could be used as the counter-argument, or one that presents a related argument, such as
    11−. Ask a pupil (one without a strip if appropriate) to select a suitable phrase or word from the
    board that could connect the two points in a piece of discursive writing. Continue with the other
    strips in the same way until they have all been discussed. Collect the strips after they have been
    read.
4 Ask the class to view the issue from the personal perspective of a town councillor, who needs to
    decide whether she or he should vote to keep the town's zoo or close it down. Hold up the card
    with the words: *I will vote to keep the zoo* written on it. Explain that the pupils will be asked to
    help the councillor make up his or her mind whether to accept this view or not, by presenting a
    balanced view of all the arguments. Explain that they will be using a drama strategy known as
    conscience alley, where the character walks around the room towards a decision on a card. As the
    character walks, the pupils put forward contrasting points of view, as if they were the character's
    conscience. If the character takes the card after listening to all the arguments, this is a sign that
    he or she will have been persuaded to accept that point of view. However, if the character refuses
    to take the card, he or she will have been persuaded of the opposite point of view. Make it clear
    that pupils may be asked to express a point of view, which is not their own. Reassure the pupils
    that they will be given an opportunity to express their own views after this activity. Explain that you
    will represent the councillor during the activity.

Development

1 Explain that the pupils sitting nearest the *For* sheet will argue for keeping zoos, and those nearest
    the *Against* sheet will argue the opposite view.
2 Allow pairs a few minutes to discuss and then record between three and five points for their given
    side of the argument. Ask pupils to ensure that their points are expressed clearly.
3 Write the numbers 1 to 6 down the side of each paper on the wall. Ask one pair to put forward
    one point of view to support the *For keeping the zoo* side and summarise this as sentence number 1

on the *For* sheet. Then ask if anyone on the *Against keeping the zoo* side has a point that would act as a counter-argument or a related argument, and write this as the corresponding sentence number 1 on the *Against* sheet. Not all points will have a counter-argument, but those that go together should be given the same number. Carry on in this way until you have at least five or six points on each sheet. Note that it will not be a problem if there are more points on one sheet than the other.

4 Allocate a different sentence to each of the pairs on each side. With larger classes, some pairs will inevitably have the same sentence. Then allow pupils a few minutes to adapt or extend their sentence, in order to make their argument more convincing. Remind pupils to phrase their points as if they were talking to the councillor. Discuss an example first if necessary, so pupils have a model to work from.

5 Pupils should write down the final version of their sentence and then decide how they will communicate the point to the councillor, for example, read it out or just explain it; read it chorally or let just one of the pair read it.

6 Now inform pupils of your route and place the decision card on the chair at the end of the route. Explain the following before you start the activity:
   ● The pupils' cue to talk is when you stop by their desk and look at them.
   ● When you move away from their desk they should stop speaking.
   ● Pupils should watch for the moment when you reach the chair with the card. This is their cue to talk again simultaneously, as if the words are now a jumble in the councillor's mind. They should continue to do this until you stop the activity by calling out *FREEZE*.

7 Once everyone is clear of the procedures, use the word *ACTION* to start. Then walk through conscience alley, listen to the arguments and make your decision. After the activity explore why some arguments were perhaps more persuasive than others.

8 Now give pupils a few minutes to record their own views on the issue with reasons.

9 Ask pupils to use the points on the sheets on the wall and the connectives on the board, to help them produce a piece of discursive writing entitled *Should We Keep Zoos?* Make it clear that this should include their own view as a conclusion. Point out the difference between speaking and writing an argument in terms of the need to compensate for the absence of non-verbal signals and a shared context in written arguments. Remind the pupils to use counter-arguments and put related points into paragraphs. Also remind pupils of the features of discussion writing by making an information sheet, or use a published resource such as *The Discussion Book* by Sue Palmer.

10 Allow the class to continue working in pairs to support each other in drafting their individual writing.

Plenary

1 Ask a few pupils to share the way they have decided to order and link the points in their writing and use this to point out good practice.

2 Inform pupils of when they will be asked to edit and complete the writing, for example, in the next lesson or for homework.

3 Remind pupils of the lesson objectives and allow pupils a few minutes in pairs to think of between one and three important things that they can remember about the work in this lesson.

4 Take brief feedback, linking the comments to the lesson objectives.

Year 7   Views on Zoos

A Drama Lesson

Main focus: Developing skills of verbal persuasion on the issue of zoos

 Links to the English Framework Objectives for Year 7

Drama:

S&L 15   develop drama techniques to explore in role a variety of situations and texts or respond to stimuli

S&L 18 develop drama techniques and strategies for anticipating, visualising and problem-solving in different learning contexts

Speaking:

S&L 5 promote, justify or defend a point of view using supporting evidence, example and illustration, which are linked back to the main argument.

Preparation

1 Fold a piece of A4 card so that it can stand up and write the words: *I will vote to keep the zoo* on the card in large letters.
2 Organise pupils into pairs and ensure they have a supply of rough paper and pencils.
3 Ensure sufficient space for pupils to stand in a curved shape and then place a chair or a table in the space.
4 Make sufficient copies of photocopiable sheet 3.1, to ensure each pair has one strip.

Introduction

1 Share the lesson objectives with the class.
2 Ask pupils to write down what they associate with the word *zoo* and then take brief feedback.
3 Give out the strips of paper from photocopiable sheet 3.1 to allocate a point of view to each pair of pupils, but keep back strip **1+**.
4 Read out strip **1+** and then ask if another pair has a strip containing a point that could be used as the counter-argument, or one that presents a related argument. Talk about how each contrasting point could be made more persuasive through evidence, example and illustration. Explain that because this is a drama lesson they will be allowed to invent anecdotes. Use point **1+** as a model and show pupils how this could be elaborated to make it more persuasive by using an anecdote.
5 Then give pairs a few minutes to invent an anecdote relating to the point on their strip or go through each point and invent anecdotes as a class.
6 Now ask the class to view the issue from the personal perspective of a town councillor, who needs to decide whether she or he should vote to keep the town's zoo open or close it down. Hold up the card with the words: *I will vote to keep the zoo* written on it. Explain that the pupils will be asked to help the councillor make up their mind whether to accept this view or not, by presenting a balanced view of all the arguments. Explain that they will be using a drama strategy known as *conscience alley*, where the character walks between two rows of pupils towards a decision on a card. As the character walks, the pupils put forward contrasting points of view, as if they were the character's conscience. If the character takes the card after listening to all the arguments, this is a sign that he or she will have been persuaded to accept that point of view. However, if the character refuses to take the card, they will have been persuaded of the opposite point of view. Make it clear that pupils will be asked to express the point of view on their strip of paper, which may or may not be their own view. Reassure the pupils that they will be given an opportunity to express their own views after the activity. Explain that you will represent the councillor during the activity.

Development

1 Give pairs of pupils a few minutes to elaborate and rehearse their verbal arguments to make them as convincing as possible. Now create conscience alley by asking pupils to stand in two rows opposite each other, to form an alleyway. With a large class it is best to make the alleyway into a curved shape, to enable all pupils to see and hear what is happening.
2 Make sure pupils understand the following points before you begin the activity:
   - You will use the word *ACTION* to start the activity and the word *FREEZE* to stop it.
   - Everyone must be silent when elected pairs are speaking. If anyone speaks out of turn you will temporarily stop the activity using the word *FREEZE*.
   - You will ask each pair to justify their arguments, as you walk down the alley.
   - Pupils should watch for the moment when you reach the chair with the card. This is their cue to talk again simultaneously, as if the words are now a jumble in the councillor's mind. They

should continue to do this until you either take hold of the card to signify that you have made the decision to keep the zoo, or call out *FREEZE*, indicating that you have decided the opposite. Make it clear that the choice will be up to you, and will be based on how well you feel the arguments have been put forward.

3　Once everyone is clear of the procedures, use the word *ACTION* to start. Then walk down conscience alley, listen to and challenge the arguments and then make your decision. After the activity explain why some arguments were perhaps more persuasive than others.

4　Now give pupils a few minutes to discuss and rehearse the arguments in support of their own views on the issue, with reasons. They can use sketches or notes if they wish. Repeat conscience alley and invite pupils to offer their own arguments as you walk through.

Plenary

1　Remind pupils of the lesson objectives and allow pupils a few minutes in pairs to think of between 1 and 3 important things that they can remember about the work in this lesson.

2　Take brief feedback, linking the comments to the lesson objectives.

Year 8　Books versus Computers

A Literacy Lesson

Main focus: Writing a discursive essay on the issue of books versus computers

Links to the English Framework Objectives for Year 8

Drama:
S&L 15　explore and develop ideas, issues and relationships through work in role
Analyse, review, comment:
TLW 16　weigh different viewpoints and present a balanced analysis of an event or issue . . .

Preparation

1　Fold a piece of A4 card so that it stands up, and write the words: *Libraries should have more computers than books* on the card in large letters.

2　Organise pupils into pairs who will sit together at the same desk, and ensure they have a supply of rough paper and pencils.

3　Plan a route around the classroom that will ensure you pass as many pairs of pupils as possible. Place an empty chair or a table at the end of the route.

4　Place a large sheet of paper on the wall at one side of the room and write the words: *For more computers* at the top in large letters. Then place another paper on the other side of the room with the words: *For more books* written on it, using a different coloured pen.

5　Write a list of suitable phrases and connectives on the blackboard, that could be used to link arguments in a discursive essay, for example: *however, it could argued that, alternatively.*

6　Make one copy of photocopiable sheet 3.2 and cut out the points in strips.

Introduction

1　Share the lesson objectives with the class.

2　Access prior learning by allowing pairs of pupils a few minutes to record between one and three arguments in favour of using computers instead of books. Then set them a second, similarly timed task, to note between one and three arguments in favour of using books instead of computers. Take brief feedback.

3　Give out the strips of paper (one per pair) from photocopiable sheet 3.2. In large classes, some pairs will not have a strip, so make it clear that everyone is expected to contribute to the discussion. Ask the pair with strip **1+** to read out their point and then ask if another pair has a point that could be used as the counter-argument, or one that presents a related argument, such as **8−**. Ask a pupil (one without a strip if appropriate) to select a suitable phrase or word from the board that could connect the two points in a piece of discursive writing. Continue with the other strips in the same way until they have all been discussed. Collect the strips after they have been read.

4   Ask the class to view the issue from the personal perspective of a librarian, who needs to decide whether she or he should devote more money to providing computers for the library than books. Hold up the card with the words: *Libraries should have more computers than books* written on it. Explain that the pupils will be asked to help the librarian make up his or her mind whether to accept this view or not, by presenting a balanced view of all the arguments. Explain that they will be using a drama strategy known as *conscience alley*, where the character walks around the room towards a decision on a card. As the character walks, the pupils put forward contrasting points of view, as if they were the character's conscience. If the character takes the card after listening to all the arguments, this is a sign that he or she will have been persuaded to accept that point of view. However, if the character refuses to take the card, he or she will have been persuaded of the opposite point of view. Make it clear that pupils may be asked to express a point of view, which is not their own. Reassure the pupils that they will be given an opportunity to express their own views after the activity. Explain that you will represent the librarian during the activity.

Development

1   Explain that the pupils sitting nearest the *For more books* sheet will argue for buying more books, and those nearest the *For more computers* sheet will argue the opposite view.

2   Allow pairs a few minutes to discuss and then record between three and five points for their given side of the argument. Ask pupils to ensure that their points are expressed clearly.

3   Ask one pair to put forward one point of view to support the *For more books* side and summarise this as sentence number 1 on the *For more books* sheet. Then ask if anyone on the *For more computers* side has a point that would act as a counter-argument or a related argument, and write this as the corresponding sentence number 1 on the *For more computers* sheet. Not all points will have a counter-argument, but those that go together should be given the same number. Carry on in this way until you have a few points on each sheet. Note that it will not be a problem if there are more points on one sheet than the other.

4   Allocate a different sentence to each of the pairs on each side. In a large class, some pairs will inevitably have the same sentence. Then allow pupils a few minutes to adapt or extend their sentence, in order to make their argument more convincing. Remind pupils to phrase their points as if they were talking to the librarian. Discuss an example first if necessary, so pupils have a model to work from.

5   Pupils should write down the final version of their sentence and then decide how they will communicate the point to the librarian, for example, read it out or just explain it; read it chorally or let just one of the pair read it.

6   Now inform pupils of your route and place the decision card on the chair at the end of the route. Explain the following before you start the activity;
   ● The pupils' cue to talk is when you stop by their desk and look at them.
   ● When you move away from their desk they should stop speaking.
   ● Pupils should watch for the moment when you reach the chair with the card. This is their cue to talk again simultaneously, as if the words are now a jumble in the librarian's mind. They should continue to do this until you either take hold of the card to signify that you have made the decision on the card, or call out *FREEZE*, indicating that you have decided the opposite. Make it clear that the choice will be up to you, and will be based on how well you feel the arguments have been put forward.

7   Once everyone is clear of the procedures, use the word *ACTION* to start. Then walk through conscience alley, listen to the arguments and make your decision. After the activity explain why some arguments were perhaps more persuasive than others.

8   Now give pupils a few minutes to record their own views on the issue with reasons.

9   Ask pupils to use the points on the sheets on the wall and the connectives on the board, to help them produce a piece of discursive writing entitled *Should Computers Replace Books?* This should include their own view as a conclusion. Point out the difference between speaking and writing an

argument in terms of the need to compensate for the absence of non-verbal signals, and a shared context in written arguments. Remind the pupils to use counter-arguments and put related points into paragraphs. Also remind pupils of the features of discursive writing by making an information sheet, or use a published resource such as *The Discussion Book* by Sue Palmer.

10 Allow the class to continue working in pairs to support each other in drafting their individual writing.

Plenary

1 Ask a few pupils to share the way they have decided to order and link the points in their writing and use this to point out good practice.

2 Inform pupils of when they will be asked to edit and complete the writing, for example, in the next lesson or for homework.

3 Allow pupils a few minutes in pairs to think of between one and three important things that they can remember about the work in this lesson.

4 Take brief feedback, linking their comments to the lesson objectives.

Year 8   Views on Books versus Computers

A Drama Lesson

Main focus: Explore the features of a balanced argument on the issue of books versus computers

Links to the English Framework Objectives for Year 8

Drama:
S&L 15   explore and develop ideas, issues and relationships through work in role
Group discussion and interaction:
S&L 10   use talk to question, hypothesise, speculate, evaluate, solve problems and develop thinking about complex issues and ideas.

Preparation

1 Fold an A4 card in half so that it stands up, and write the words: *I will spend more on computers for the library* on the card in large letters.

2 Organise pupils into pairs and ensure they have a supply of rough paper and pencils.

3 Ensure sufficient space for pupils to stand in a crescent shape. Place a chair or a table in the space.

4 Make sufficient copies of photocopiable sheet 3.2, to ensure each pair has one strip.

Introduction

1 Share the lesson objectives with the class.

2 Allow pairs a few minutes to note down between one and three arguments in favour of using computers rather than books. Then set the groups a similar timed task to note between one and three arguments in favour of using books. Take brief feedback on both arguments.

3 Give out the strips of paper from photocopiable sheet 3.2 to allocate a point of view to each pair of pupils, but keep back strip **1+**. Read out strip **1+** and then ask if another pair has a point that could be used as the counter-argument, or one that presents a related argument, such as **8−**. Talk about how each contrasting point could be made more persuasive through evidence, example and illustration. Explain that, because this is a drama lesson they will be allowed to invent anecdotes. Use point **1+** as a model and show pupils how this could be elaborated to make it more convincing.

4 Then give pairs a few minutes to elaborate and/or invent an anecdote relating to their own point. Take some feedback by asking pupils to present their arguments to the class.

5 Ask the class to view the issue from the personal perspective of a librarian, who needs to decide whether he or she should spend more money on computers than on new books in the library. Hold

up the card with the words: *I will spend more on computers for the library* written on it. Explain that the pupils will be asked to help the librarian make up their mind whether to accept this view or not, by presenting a balanced view of all the arguments. Explain that they will be using a drama strategy known as *conscience alley*, where the character walks between two rows of pupils towards a decision on a card. As the character walks, the pupils put forward contrasting points of view, as if they were the character's conscience. If the character takes the card after listening to all the arguments, this is a sign that he or she will have been persuaded to accept that point of view. However, if the character refuses to take the card, he or she will have been persuaded of the opposite point of view. Make it clear that pupils will be asked to express the point of view on their strip of paper, which may or may not be their own view. Reassure the pupils that they will be given an opportunity to express their own views after the activity. Explain that you will represent the librarian during the activity.

Development

1 Give pairs of pupils a few minutes to elaborate and rehearse their verbal arguments to make them as convincing as possible. Now create conscience alley by asking pupils to stand in two rows opposite each other, to form an alleyway. With a large class it is best to make the alleyway into a curved shape, to enable all pupils to see and hear what is happening.

2 Make sure pupils understand the following points before you begin the activity:
  ● You will use the word *ACTION* to start the activity and the word *FREEZE* to stop.
  ● Everyone must be silent when elected pairs are speaking. If anyone speaks out of turn you will temporarily stop the activity using the word *FREEZE*.
  ● You will ask each pair to justify their arguments, as you walk down the alley.
  ● Pupils should watch for the moment when you reach the chair with the card. This is their cue to talk again simultaneously, as if the words are now a jumble in the librarian's mind. They should continue to do this until you either take hold of the card to signify that you have made the decision on the card, or call out *FREEZE*, indicating that you have decided the opposite. Make it clear that the choice will be up to you, and will be based on how well you feel the arguments have been put forward.

3 Once everyone is clear of the procedures, use the word *ACTION* to start. Then walk down conscience alley, listen to and challenge the arguments and then make your decision. After the activity explain why some arguments were perhaps more persuasive than others.

4 Now give pupils a few minutes to discuss and rehearse the arguments in support of their own views on the issue, with reasons. They can use sketches or notes if they wish. Repeat conscience alley and invite pupils to offer their own arguments as you walk through.

Plenary

1 Allow pupils a few minutes in pairs to note between one and three important things that they can remember about the work in this lesson.

2 Take brief feedback, linking the pupils comments to the lesson objectives.

Year 9   Verdict on the Media

A Literacy Lesson

Main focus: Writing a discursive essay on the issue of whether the media is guilty of misconduct

 Links to the English Framework Objectives for Year 9

Drama:
S&L 12   use a range of drama techniques, including work in role, to explore issues, ideas and meanings . . .

Analyse, review, comment:
TLW 16   present a balanced analysis of a situation, text, issue or set of ideas, taking into account a range of evidence and opinions.

Preparation

1 Fold two pieces of A4 card so they stand up. Write the words: *The media is GUILTY of misconduct* on one of the cards, and *The media is NOT GUILTY of misconduct* on the other card.

2 Organise pupils into pairs who will sit together at the same desk, and ensure they have a supply of rough paper and pencils.

3 Plan a route around the classroom that will ensure you pass as many pairs of pupils as possible. Place an empty chair or a table at the end of the route.

4 Place a large sheet of paper on the wall at one side of the room and write the words: *The media is GUILTY of misconduct* at the top in large letters. Then place another paper on the other side of the room and write the words: *The media is NOT GUILTY of misconduct* on it, using a different coloured pen.

5 Write a list of suitable phrases and connectives on the blackboard, that could be used to link arguments in a discursive essay, for example: *however, it could argued that, alternatively.*

6 Make one copy of photocopiable sheet 3.3, and cut out the points in strips.

Introduction

1 Share the lesson objectives with the class.

2 Make sure that pupils understand that for the purposes of this lesson the term 'media' refers to: TV, radio, videos, films, newspapers and magazines and so on.

3 Access prior learning by holding a brief discussion to collect initial ideas on whether the media should be guilty or not guilty of misconduct.

4 Give out the strips of paper (one per pair) from photocopiable sheet 3.3. In large classes, some pairs will not have a strip, so make it clear that everyone is expected to contribute to the discussion. Ask the pair with strip **1+** to read out their point, and then ask if another pair has a point that could be used as the counter-argument, or one that presents a related argument, such as **8−**. Ask a pupil (one without a strip if appropriate) to select a suitable phrase or word from the board that could connect the two points in a piece of discursive writing. Continue with the other strips in the same way until they have all been discussed. Collect the strips after they have been read.

5 Ask the class to imagine that the media has been personified and put on trial for misconduct. Explain that, near the end of the lesson, the class will be asked to decide whether media is guilty or not guilty of misconduct. Hold up the two verdict cards with *The media is GUILTY of misconduct* and *The media is NOT GUILTY of misconduct* written on them. Explain that the jury will be asked to make up their mind, by considering a balanced view of all the arguments. Explain that in order to consider all the arguments, they will use a drama strategy known as *conscience alley*, where a member of the jury walks around the room towards the two verdict cards. As the person walks, the pupils put forward the contrasting points of view, as if they were the person's conscience. The jury member takes the card that best fits his or her opinion, after considering all the arguments. Make it clear that, in this part of the exercise, pupils may be asked to express a point of view which is not their own. Reassure the pupils that they will be given an opportunity to express their own views after the activity. Explain that you will represent the jury member during the conscience alley activity, so they can concentrate on the arguments. However, make it clear that the final verdict will depend on the class' majority vote.

Development

1 Explain that the pupils sitting nearest the *NOT GUILTY* sheet will argue that the media is not guilty of misconduct, and those nearest the *GUILTY* sheet will argue the guilty view.

2 Allow pairs a few minutes to discuss and then record between three and five points for their given side of the argument. Ask pupils to ensure that their points are expressed clearly.

3 Ask one pair to put forward one point of view to support the *GUILTY* side. Summarise this as sentence number 1 on the *GUILTY* sheet. Then ask if anyone on the *NOT GUILTY* side has a point that would act as a counter-argument or a related argument. Write this as the corresponding sentence number 1 on the *NOT GUILTY* sheet. Not all points will have a counter-argument, but

those that go together should be given the same number. Carry on in this way until you have a few points on each sheet. Note that it will not be a problem if there are more points on one sheet than the other.

4   Allocate the sentences to all the pairs on each side. In large classes some pairs will inevitably have the same sentence. Then allow pupils a few minutes to adapt or extend their sentence, in order to make their argument more convincing. Remind pupils to phrase their points as if they were talking to the jury member. Discuss an example first if necessary, so pupils have a model to work from.

5   Pupils should write down their final version, and then decide how they will communicate the point to the member of the jury, for example: read it out or just explain it; read it chorally or let just one of the pair read it.

6   Now inform pupils of your route and place the decision cards on the chair at the end of the route. Explain the following before you start the activity:
   ● The pupils' cue to talk is when you stop by their desk and look at them.
   ● When you move away from their desk they should stop speaking.
   ● Pupils should watch for the moment when you reach the chair with the cards. This is their cue to talk again simultaneously, as if the words are now a jumble in the person's mind. They should continue to do this until you take hold of one of the cards to signify that you have made your decision. Make it clear that the choice will be up to you, and will be based on how well you feel the arguments have been put forward.

7   Once everyone is clear of the procedures, use the word *ACTION* to start. Then walk through conscience alley, listen to the arguments and make your decision. After the activity explain why some arguments were more persuasive than others.

8   Now give pupils a few minutes to note down their own views on the issue. Encourage pupils to back up their points with valid reasons.

9   Ask pupils to use the points on the sheets on the wall and the connectives on the board to help them produce a piece of discursive writing entitled: *Is the Media Guilty of Misconduct?* This should include their own view as a conclusion. Remind the pupils to use counter-arguments and put related points into paragraphs. If necessary, remind pupils of the features of discursive writing by making an information sheet, or use a published resource such as *The Discussion Book* by Sue Palmer.

10 Allow the class to continue working in pairs to support each other in drafting their individual writing.

Plenary

1   Ask pupils to take on the role of the jury and vote on whether they think the media is guilty or not guilty of misconduct.
2   Inform pupils of when they will be asked to edit and complete the writing, for example, in the next lesson or for homework.
3   Remind pupils of the lesson objectives and allow pupils 2 minutes in pairs to think of between one and three important things that they can remember about the work in this lesson.
4   Take brief feedback, linking pupils' comments to the lesson objectives.

Year 9   Opinions on the Media

A Drama Lesson

Main focus: Discuss and evaluate conflicting opinions on the issue of whether the media is guilty of misconduct

. . . .

 Links to the English Framework Objectives for Year 9

Drama:
S&L 12   use a range of drama techniques, including work in role, to explore issues, ideas and meanings . . .

Speaking:
S&L 2   use standard English to explain, explore or justify an idea
Group discussion and interaction:
S&L 9   discuss and evaluate conflicting evidence to arrive at a considered viewpoint.

Preparation

1 Fold two sheets of A4 cards so they stand up, and write the words: *The media is GUILTY of misconduct* on one of the cards, and *The media is NOT GUILTY of misconduct* on the other card.

2 Organise pupils into pairs and ensure they have a supply of rough paper and pencils.

3 Ensure sufficient space for all pupils to stand in a curved formation and place two chairs or tables at opposite sides of the room.

4 Make sufficient copies of photocopiable sheet 3.3, to ensure each pair has one strip.

Introduction

1 Share the lesson objectives with the class.

2 Make sure that pupils understand that, for the purposes of this lesson, the term media refers to: TV, radio, videos, films, newspapers and magazines, and so on.

3 Briefly discuss general points for and against the media to access prior learning.

4 Ask the class to imagine that the media has been personified and put on trial for misconduct. Explain that, near the end of the lesson, the class are to be the jury and will decide by majority vote whether the media is guilty or not guilty of misconduct. Then the jury will be asked to make up their mind, by considering a balanced view of all the arguments. Explain that in order to consider all the arguments, they will use a drama strategy known as *conscience alley*, where the judge will walk between two rows of pupils who argue points as councils for the defence and the prosecution. As the judge walks, the pupils put forward the contrasting points of view as if they were in court. Make it clear that pupils may be asked to express a point of view, which is not their own. Reassure the pupils that they will be given an opportunity to express their own views after the activity. Explain that you will represent the judge during the conscience alley activity, so the pupils can concentrate on the arguments. However, make it clear that the final verdict will depend on the class' majority vote.

5 Give out the strips of paper from photocopiable sheet 3.3 to allocate a point of view to pairs of pupils, but keep back strip **1+**. Read out strip **1+** and then ask if another pair has a point that could be used as the counter-argument, or one that presents a related argument, such as **8−**. Talk about how each point could be made more convincing through evidence, example and illustration.

6 Explain that, because this is a drama lesson they will be allowed to invent anecdotes if appropriate. Use point **1+** as a model and show pupils how this could be elaborated to make it more convincing. Emphasise that they should use standard English, as if they were councils presenting arguments in court. Discuss some appropriate phrases for court if necessary.

Development

1 Allow pairs a few minutes to prepare and rehearse their arguments for the judge. Then take some feedback by asking a few pupils to present their arguments to the class.

2 Now create conscience alley by asking pupils to stand in two rows opposite each other, to form an alleyway. With a large class it is best to make the alleyway into a curved shape, to enable all pupils to see and hear what is happening.

3 Make sure pupils understand the following points before you begin the activity:
   ● You will use the word *ACTION* to start the activity and the word *FREEZE* to stop.
   ● Pairs will be invited to speak in turn by the judge.
   ● Everyone must be silent when elected pairs are speaking. If anyone speaks out of turn you will temporarily stop the activity using the word *FREEZE*.
   ● The judge may ask each pair further questions to clarify their arguments for the jury.

4 Once everyone is clear about the procedures, walk down conscience alley, listen to the arguments and seek clarification or elaboration if necessary. Stop the activity mid-way if pupils have

problems with using standard English, and discuss how they can adapt their language before starting again.

5   After the activity, talk about why you found some arguments more convincing than others.

6   Now ask each pair to join another pair forming groups of four. Allow the groups a few minutes to discuss the arguments before coming to their own conclusions about whether the media is guilty or not guilty of misconduct. Instruct groups to organise themselves so that everyone has the opportunity to express their own point of view.

Plenary

1   Place the *GUILTY* card on the chair on one side of the room and the *NOT GUILTY* card on the chair on the opposite side. Ask pupils to vote on whether they think the media is guilty or not guilty of misconduct by standing by the appropriate card. Count the pupils by each card to obtain a majority verdict.

2   Allow pupils a few minutes in pairs to consider between one and three important things that they can remember about the work in this lesson.

3   Take brief feedback, linking the pupils' comments to the lesson objectives.

UNIT FOUR   MIME AND ACTIONS

Making Links

Links to the National Curriculum Key Stages 3 and 4 English Programmes of Study:

Drama: **S&L 4**   To participate in a range of drama activities and to evaluate their own and others' contributions, pupils should be taught to use a variety of dramatic techniques to explore ideas, issues, texts and meanings.

Links to the English Framework Objectives

Year 7
Drama: **S&L 18**
Sentence construction and punctuation: **Sn 7**

Year 8
Drama: **S&L 15**
Vocabulary: **Wd 7c**
Standard English and language variation: **Sn 13**

Year 9
Drama: **S&L 12**

Links to Schemes of Work

Punctuation; Language from a different historical period

Links to specific texts

Year 7   *The Switch* by Anthony Horowitz
Year 8   *A Midsummer Night's Dream* by William Shakespeare
Year 9   *Twelfth Night* by William Shakespeare

Definition

Mime in the context of this unit is taken to mean the non-verbal portrayal of a physical action such as sweeping the floor or washing.

Actions refer to more symbolic movements, such as those representing the meaning of a word or the shape of a punctuation mark.

Teaching and Learning Rationale

Mime and the use of symbolic action are dramatic techniques that can be useful performance skills in their own right. However, in this unit they are employed as effective teaching strategies to support aspects of reading and writing.

The visual and kinaesthetic nature of both observing and performing mimes and actions helps pupils explore, understand and recall challenging concepts and vocabulary. In order to represent something symbolically through mime or action, pupils must seek to fully understand the nature of what it is they are required to represent. The interactive nature of mime and action also makes them suitable strategies for a literacy lesson starter activity.

Year 7   The Punctuation Challenge

A Literacy Lesson Starter Activity

Main focus: Punctuation – integrating speech into larger sentences

Links to specific text *The Switch* by Anthony Horowitz

Links to the English Framework Objectives for Year 7

Drama:

S&L 18   develop drama techniques and strategies for anticipating, visualising and problem-solving in different learning contexts

Sentence construction and punctuation:

Sn 7   use speech punctuation accurately to integrate speech into larger sentences.

Preparation

1   You will need access to a black or a white board.
2   Organise pupils into mixed ability pairs.
3   Make one copy of each of photocopiable sheets 4.1 and 4.2. Cut up each of the photocopiable sheets along the dotted lines provided. Enlarge the sections if necessary and either laminate them or place them in individual plastic pockets.
4   Make one copy of photocopiable sheet 4.3 for each pair of pupils.
5   Make one copy of each of photocopiable sheets 4.4 and 4.5. Cut up each of the photocopiable sheets along the dotted lines provided. Enlarge the sections if necessary and either laminate them or place in individual plastic pockets.
6   Clear a space towards the front or round the edge of the room, large enough for 15 pupils to stand in a straight or curved line.

Introduction

1   Share the relevant lesson objectives with the class.
2   Introduce the activity as *The Punctuation Challenge*.
3   Distribute the sections of photocopiable sheets 4.1 and 4.2 among six pupils and ask them to stand in any order in the allocated space. They should hold the sections of the sheets in front of them, so that the class can read the words.
4   Ask the class to suggest the correct order for the sections. Avoid everyone calling out suggestions by asking volunteers to take turns to move the sections around until the majority of the class agree on the final order.
5   Inform the class of the correct order and adjust the line-up if necessary.
6   Point to each section in the correct order and ask the whole class to read the words chorally as you point. Insist that they wait for you to point to the appropriate section before they attempt to read it.

Development

1   Indicate that the punctuation is missing from the sentences. Challenge the class to put in the correct punctuation marks, one at a time. Start by asking one of the pupils to suggest *one* of the punctuation marks that would appear in this passage and then carry out the same procedure for the rest of the punctuation marks.
2   Ask the pupil who made the suggestion to come to the front and stand in the place where that punctuation mark would appear. For example, there would be a full stop at the end of the first sentence on photocopiable sheet 4.1, so the pupil would stand to the right of the pupil holding that sentence, as viewed by the class. Ask the class for their opinion and ensure that this is correct.

3 Explain that, after all the punctuation marks have been added in this way, the class will be asked to read the passage again in chorus, but this time they will also read out the names of the punctuation marks as they occur. Explain that when you point to a pupil representing a punctuation mark, two things will happen:
  ● The class will call out the *name* of the mark i.e. full stop, comma, opening speech marks, closing speech marks, question mark, exclamation mark.
  ● The pupil representing the mark will *perform an action* to represent the mark. Explain that you will demonstrate or explain each of the different actions (see below) as the pupils suggest them. Use the following actions or make up your own:

Full stop – *stamp one foot*

Comma – *take one step diagonally and sway slightly to and fro*

Opening speech marks – *turn sideways. Arch both arms above the head of the pupil holding the next sheet, to make the shape, of inverted commas.*

Closing speech marks – *turn sideways (the reverse of opening speech marks). Arch both arms above the head of the pupil holding the last sheet, to make the shape of inverted commas.*

Question mark – *make the arched shape of the top of a question mark by curving the arms above the head. Stand straight to represent the stem, and make a small jump with feet together to represent the dot underneath.*

Exclamation mark – *stand straight and put both arms in the air with palms together to represent the stem. Make a small jump with feet together to represent the dot underneath.*

FULL STOP   COMMA   OPENING SPEECH MARKS

CLOSING SPEECH MARKS   QUESTION MARK   EXCLAMATION MARK

Use this activity to revise the functions of basic punctuation marks and the rules of their usage.

4 When all the punctuation marks have been included correctly and the pupils understand their actions, point along the line of pupils and ask the class to respond chorally as explained. If carried out correctly, the passage should be read out in the following way:

After two days as evacuees we ran away / **full stop** / We thumbed a lift and then walked the rest of the way home / **full stop** / My Gran opened the door and nearly fainted / **full stop** / **opening speech marks** / What are you two doing here / **question mark** / **closing speech marks** / she said / **full stop** / **opening speech marks** / Your Mum will kill you / **exclamation mark** / **closing speech marks** / **full stop**

5 Ask the pupils at the front to return to their seats. Then give out one copy of photocopiable sheet 4.3 per pair of pupils and give them a few minutes to complete Task 1. Whilst pupils are completing this, write the passage on the board, *without* the punctuation marks.

6 Stop the activity. Fill in the correct punctuation marks on the passage on the board and ask pupils to check their answers.

7 Ask pairs to complete Task 2 on photocopiable sheet 4.3 in preparation for another *Punctuation Challenge* line-up based on the text in Task 2 which has been adapted from *The Switch* by Anthony Horowitz.

8 Whilst pupils work on this, copy Task 2 onto the board, *without* the punctuation marks.

9 Give the sections of photocopiable sheets 4.4 and 4.5 to eight different pupils and repeat *The Punctuation Challenge* line-up as before.
Fill in the correct punctuation marks on the passage on the board as you discuss each mark.

10 The corrected passage is printed below:

> **He turned to Spurling, who was standing beside him. 'Have you poured me a brandy Spurling?'**
>
> **'Yes, Sir Hubert.'**
>
> **'Well you can drink it for me too. I haven't got time.'**
>
> **Taking the glass the chauffeur bowed and left the room.**

Check that pupils have put in the correct punctuation before they begin the choral reading as in the previous activity.

11 Link this starter activity to the relevant lesson objective.

Year 8   Midsummer Dream

A Literacy Lesson

Main focus: Developing pupils' knowledge and understanding of Shakespeare's language

Link to specific text   *A Midsummer Night's Dream* by William Shakespeare

Links to the English Framework Objectives for Year 8

Drama:
S&L 15   explore and develop ideas, issues and relationships through work in role
Vocabulary:
Wd 7c   understand and explain exactly what words mean in particular contexts
Standard English and language variation:
Sn 13   recognise some of the differences in sentence structure, vocabulary and tone between a modern English text and a text from another historical period.

Preparation

1 This lesson works best where the pupils have some prior knowledge of the storyline of *A Midsummer Night's Dream* by William Shakespeare.

2 In the drama lesson version, you will need a space for pupils to move around freely.

3 Organise the pupils into pairs, and either give each pair access to rough paper and writing materials, or use a central flipchart or white board (see Plenary below).

4 Give one highlighter pen to each pair of pupils (optional).

5 Make sufficient copies of the extract from *A Midsummer Night's Dream* on photocopiable sheet 4.6 (at least one copy per pair of pupils).

6 Make sufficient copies of the definitions on photocpiable sheets 4.7a and 4.7b.

Introduction

1 Share the objectives of the lesson with the class.

2 Distribute at least one copy of photocopiable sheet 4.6 per pair of pupils and *briefly* explain the context of this extract and a summary of the overall meaning.

3 Read the extract to the pupils, but warn them beforehand that they are unlikely to understand all the words, because they are from another historical period. Ask the pupils to locate the words 'Contagious fogs' in the extract and discuss its meaning as a phrase in its own right.

4 Ask the pupils to help you invent an action or a simple set of movements that would represent these two words. This is likely to involve reaching out arms with outspread fingers to represent 'contagious' and some move to indicate restricted vision in relation to the 'fog'. Ask all pupils to demonstrate the movement as they all say the words 'Contagious fog' aloud.

5 Individual pupils should then select one of the underlined words or phrases and invent an action or a simple movement to represent that word or phrase. Encourage pupils to choose words they understand.

6 Pupils should then work in pairs to teach each other their respective words and associated actions.

7 Ask a few pairs to feedback to the class by demonstrating their actions as you read their selected words.

Development

1 Read the text to the class again and explain that the rest of the lesson will involve preparing to understand and then perform the underlined words as you read the text aloud. Explain that the whole class will perform the underlined words in the first and last lines and the rest will be shared out among pairs of pupils.

2 Use a dictionary and/or the definitions on photocopiable sheets 4.7a and 4.7b to help the class devise movements for the underlined words in the first and last lines. Now read the lines slowly as the class carry out the agreed actions for the underlined words.

3 Then allocate a few lines to each pair to work out actions and perform, so that the class can perform as much of the extract as possible. Inevitably, small classes will only perform part of the extract and large classes will need to be given fewer lines per pair. It may be useful to keep back a few lines for those who finish before the others or give more able pairs more lines to perform. If you have access to highlighters allow pupils to mark their particular lines.

4 Allow pairs some time to invent their movements and encourage them to use a copy of photocopiable sheets 4.7a and 4.7b and/or dictionaries to discover the correct meanings of the words.

5 Remind the pupils of the context and the overall meaning of this extract. Then read the text through slowly, allowing sufficient time for the pupils to perform the underlined words and phrases. It may be useful to perform this twice.

Plenary

1 Remind the pupils of the lesson objectives and allow pupils a few minutes in pairs to identify between 3 and 5 words or phrases from the extract that we are less likely to use today, when writing modern English. Then take brief feedback and use this to point up a very brief discussion on the way language has, and continues to, change.

2   Review the learning by asking pupils to suggest images connected with this extract, such as: fat crows, fogs, muddy fields, fountains and mazes. Then either ask each pair to use these images to create a collection of sketches, or a word collage to represent the extract, or to create a whole-class version on a flipchart or white board.

Year 9 Shakespeare – The Silent Movie

A Literacy Lesson

Main focus: Developing awareness of the main events in Act 1 of *Twelfth Night* by William Shakespeare

This strategy can also be applied to another Act or Scene in this or any other play.

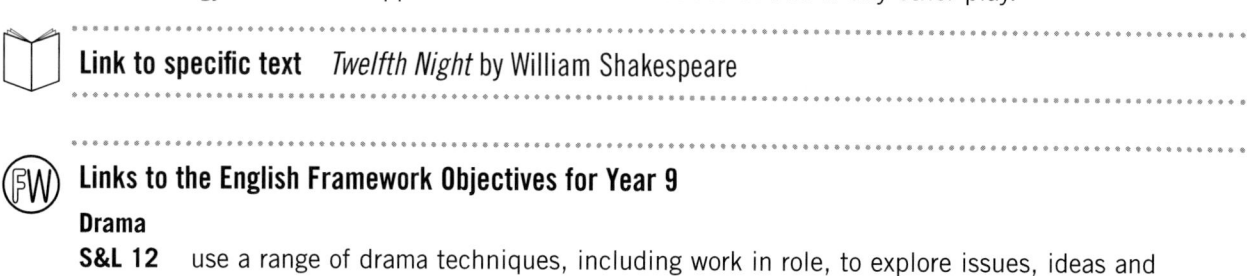

Link to specific text   *Twelfth Night* by William Shakespeare

Links to the English Framework Objectives for Year 9

Drama

S&L 12   use a range of drama techniques, including work in role, to explore issues, ideas and meanings . . .

Preparation

1   This lesson works best where pupils are relatively unfamiliar with the main events of the play.
2   Create a performance space at the front of, or in the centre of the class.
3   Make one copy of photocopiable sheet 4.8 and make individual name tags or sticky labels for each character in the chosen scene.
4   For a differentiated version – provide pupils with one copy of the text per pair.

Introduction

1   Share the lesson objective with the class and add an additional objective of helping the class to become familiar with the opening scenes of the play.
2   Explain that some pupils will be asked to walk through the main events in the scenes, as if they were in a silent movie but without the characteristic rapid movements. Use the name tags to allocate pupils to the characters and ask them to sit or stand near the performance area, ready to perform.
3   Explain that the characters should react appropriately to your fairly rapid reading of the main events, by walking the moves and using brief actions or mime.
4   Read out the main events on photocopiable sheet 4.8 and ask pupils to respond by performing as if it were a silent movie. This will be a little chaotic at first so you will need to run a rehearsal followed by a final version. This is meant to be fairly lighthearted and should not involve paying much attention to acting skills or accuracy of mime. The main purpose of this activity is to enable the pupils to see the events unfold rapidly, so that a sense of the whole of Act 1 can be retained in the memory for later study. This method caters for those pupils who learn best through visual and kinaesthetic teaching methods.

An alternative version with more challenge

1   Organise pupils into small groups.
2   Select another part of the play and divide it into sections of about 100 lines per section.
3   Allocate one section to each group.

Differentiation

Either

a) give each group a summary of their section to practice and then perform a silent movie version

or

b) ask each group to summarise their section themselves. They should describe what is happening in fairly short sentences. The sentences should answer the questions: *Where is it set? Who is there? What do they do?*

As an extension task for either of the above, ask the groups to decide how their section might be staged in terms of set, costume and lighting, together with reasons for their choice.

Plenary

1 Ask pupils quick questions to test their memory of the main events in Act 1.
2 Link the work to the objectives of the lesson.

UNIT FIVE   VARIATIONS ON HOT-SEATING

Making Links

Links to the National Curriculum Key Stages 3 and 4 English Programmes of Study

Drama: **S&L 4**   To participate in a range of drama activities and to evaluate their own and others' contributions, pupils should be taught to use a variety of dramatic techniques to explore ideas, issues, texts and meanings.

Links to the English Framework Objectives

Year 7
Drama: **S&L 15, 17**
Reading for meaning: **TLR 6**
Persuade, argue, advise: **TLW 17**

Year 8
Drama: **S&L 15**
Persuade, argue, advise: **TLW 15**

Year 9
Drama: **S&L 12, 13**

Links to Schemes of Work

The Novel; The Play; Shakespeare

Links to specific texts

Year 7   *Skellig* by David Almond
Year 8   *Holes* by Louis Sachar
Year 9   *Twelfth Night* by William Shakespeare

Definition

The traditional version

Hot-seating traditionally refers to the strategy of asking one person to sit on a chair known as the hot-seat, which is positioned at the front of the class. When this person sits in the hot-seat they take on the role of a specified character from a text. The group then ask this character questions relating to events and to other characters in the text.

Variations

1   A few pupils sit at the front to represent a number of *different* characters from the same text.
      These characters are hot-seated together. Decide beforehand whether each character should be allowed to respond to what the other characters are saying during the hot-seating.
2   A *group* of pupils sit at the front of the class to represent *one* character.
      Whenever a pupil speaks he or she represents the voice of the selected character.
3   *Several* pupils can be hot-seated in role as *people associated* with a central character or characters.
      For example their relatives, friends, fellow pupils or colleagues, teachers, neighbours or eye-witnesses to an event in the text.

4   *Half the class can hot-seat the other half* in role as a group with some information about the central character.

   For example, half the class can devise questions as reporters, who are interviewing the other half, in role as pupils who attend the same school as the central character. The teacher then acts as chair to the proceedings.

5   *During the reading of a text*, groups of pupils are allocated a character.

   The teacher interrupts the reading at significant points to ask each group to respond and answer questions from the perspective of their character.

Questioning

During the hot-seating the class can ask questions:

- as themselves
- in role as an interested party, such as reporters or investigators
- in role as minor characters within the text.

Organisation

- Pupils can ask questions spontaneously.
- Pupils can work in pairs and be allowed time to devise between three and five questions before the hot-seating.
- The whole class can work out the first few questions and allocate these to individual pupils who will ask them during the hot-seating.
- The teacher can prepare the first few questions beforehand, writing them on cards which will be given to individual pupils to read out during the hot-seating.
- Before the hot-seating begins, decide which pupils will ask the first few questions and agree on *hands up* or another signal to indicate a desire to ask a question.

Teaching and Learning Rationale

Hot-seating meets the needs of pupils who prefer to learn through visual and kinaesthetic learning styles. It can be a powerful tool in helping pupils to empathise with a character or gain a deeper understanding of the consequences of events in a text. It also brings pupils closer to the text by making the events come alive through the eyes of a character. This can also support writing-in-role in forms such as diaries, letters or writing advice to the character. However, you need to be clear about why you are using hot-seating and ensure that the character in the hot-seat is the one who can best fulfil your objective. Some main characters may not be the ones to put in the hot-seat because they cannot give a perspective which will challenge the thinking of the group. In some texts, a main character may prove to be so unpopular that it would be difficult for the class to respond to that character without prejudice and pupils may react in an extreme manner. In this case, it may be better to hot-seat someone else who can communicate events from the perspective of that character, such as a neighbour, relative or friend.

Hot-seating can provide opportunities for pupils to develop their questioning skills but they usually need support to devise appropriately focused questions. This provides a real reason for looking at questioning skills and provides an opportunity for pupils to consider questions in relation to audience and purpose.

Whilst the traditional method of hot-seating can be successful, it has the potential to be problematic. The traditional way relies on the knowledge and understanding of the person in the hot-seat. If this is the teacher, or a knowledgeable pupil then this can work well, but it can also be risky. The whole exercise relies on the integrity of the person in the hot-seat and the way in which the exercise is introduced. If pupils do not take it seriously, or use it as an opportunity to subvert the lesson, then hot-seating will not work. The pupils in the hot-seat therefore need to be carefully selected and the exercise needs to be introduced with integrity. Pupils asking the questions also require guidance in order to ensure that their questions are appropriate and taken seriously.

Setting up hot-seating as teacher-in-role

If pupils are new to hot-seating it may be best to model the process by sitting on the hot-seat yourself. This will act as a good model for the integrity of a role and enable you to have more control of the exercise. However this needs to be set up carefully beforehand by asking the class to accept that you will represent the character. It is rare that pupils do not agree to this, but should a pupil refuse to accept you in role for any reason, then just ask them not to take part for the duration of the hot-seating. The pupil will benefit from listening but will not take part in the questioning.

Use a simple item of clothing such as a scarf or shawl to indicate that you are in role and use the words *ACTION* and *FREEZE* to start and stop the hot-seating. It is advisable to let the class know this beforehand. This makes it absolutely clear when you are in role and when you are not. These clear signs of role allow you to temporarily abort the process for any reason, should the need arise.

Before you sit in the hot-seat, decide which pupils will ask the first few questions and decide how the pupils will indicate that they want to ask a question. *Hands up* is usual but there can be other signs. If pupils call out, then stop the hot-seating and bring the problem to their attention with a reminder to take turns or wait until the character invites them to speak.

Role on the wall to access prior learning and review

Before the pupils consider their questions for the hot-seating, draw an outline of the character on a flipchart or board, or alternatively, draw a circle containing the name of the character or group of characters who are to be hot-seated. Leave some space outside the outline or circle. Access prior learning by asking pupils what they already know about the character(s) from the text and record these responses inside the outline or circle.

Return to this outline during the plenary. Remind pupils what they said they *knew* about the character(s) from the text and ask them what they now *think* about the character(s) as a result of the hot-seating. Record what they *think* outside the outline and compare the two views.

Step by Step Overview

METHOD: An individual pupil or a teacher represents a character

Preparation

1 Decide on the purpose of the hot-seating and select an appropriate character or characters for the hot-seat.
2 Clear a space at the front of the class with chairs for the hot-seat(s).
3 Select an appropriate item of clothing to represent the character if you are to use teacher-in-role.
4 If more than two characters are to be hot-seated together, write a name tag or adhesive label for each character to wear.
5 Decide on how the class will be supported to ask questions and write a few questions on cards if appropriate.
6 Provide pupils with rough paper and writing materials if they will be devising their own questions.
7 Obtain the use of a flipchart or a whiteboard. Draw an outline of the character(s) who will be in the hot-seat or draw a circle containing their name on the flipchart or board. Allow space outside the outline or circle.

Introduction

1 Share the lesson objective with the class and outline the strategy and its purpose.
2 Select the character or characters to be in the hot-seat and use the name tags or clothing if appropriate.
3 Access prior learning by asking pupils what they already know about the character(s) from the text and record their responses on the inside of the outline or circle on the flipchart or white board.
4 Prepare pupils to ask questions from the options suggested previously.
5 Agree on signs for when the hot-seating will start and stop and agree on how it will proceed in terms of asking and answering questions.
6 If you intend to work as teacher-in-role, ask the class to accept you in role as the character for the duration of the hot-seating.
7 Select a few pupils to ask the first few questions to start off the process.

Development

1 Invite the character(s) to take the hot-seat and let the first few pupils ask their questions.
2 After the elected pupils have asked their questions, allow others to ask theirs.
3 Let the hot-seating proceed until you have achieved your objective. If you are working as teacher-in-role, concentrate on presenting an attitude rather than giving a performance. Try not to behave in a manner that is vastly different from how you would normally speak and react, as this can make it difficult for pupils to take the exercise seriously.
4 Stop the hot-seating and allow pupils a short time in pairs to summarise what they have found out from the character(s).
5 Take feedback and use this as a basis for discussion.

Plenary

Role on the wall

Return to the outline of the character or the circle on the white board or flipchart. Remind the class what they said they *knew* about the character from the text prior to the lesson. Now ask the class what they *think* about the character(s) after the hot-seating and record their responses outside the outline or circle. If appropriate, use this to help the class distinguish between factual evidence as revealed in the text and opinion, and to identify opinions based on inference and deduction.

Remind the class of the lesson objectives and link to the contents of this lesson.

Other Variations

VARIATION 1: Several pupils represent one character

Proceed as above with the following adaptations:

Preparation

Place several chairs in the hot-seating space.

Introduction

Explain the concept that when one of the hot-seating group speaks, they represent the voice of the chosen character. Make it clear that members of the group should not contradict each other in terms of factual information, for example, if one of the group maintains that they went to town last Friday to buy a new coat, then another member cannot claim they stayed in all day. If this should occur then stop the hot-seating and come to some agreement as to which fact will be accepted.

Development

1 Take on the role of a chairperson to organise which pupils from the class will ask questions and which member of the hot-seating group will respond to the questions as the character. Try to ensure that each member of the hot-seating group has an opportunity to respond.
2 If members of the hot-seating group appear to differ in their responses as the character, stop the process and use this as an opportunity to ask the class how they think the character should respond. The final response will need to be negotiated, or set in the context that one response will have to be selected for the purposes of the hot-seating, despite other responses being as valid.

VARIATION 2: Several pupils represent people associated with a central character or characters

Preparation

1 Place one chair per central character in the hot-seating space. Avoid more than two characters.
2 Select a suitable whole-group role for the class, in terms of people who know something about the central character(s).
3 **Option A** Use other characters from a text to explore their relationships with the central character(s).

If there are more pupils in the class than characters, allocate one character to pairs or groups. For example, in *Macbeth*, the central characters would be Macbeth and Lady Macbeth and groups or pairs would represent each of the other characters in the play, including the minor characters (see point 1 below for optional preparatory task).

4 **Option B** Create interested parties who would have an opinion on the central character(s), such as relatives, friends, fellow pupils or colleagues, teachers, neighbours or eye-witnesses to an event involving the central character(s).

Introduction

Option A: Working with all the minor characters in a text

1 Before starting the hot-seating, allow pupils time to work in pairs or small groups to consider how their character feels about the central character(s), based on what they know or can deduce from the text. This could be a homework task in preparation for the lesson. Allow the pupil(s) playing the central character(s) the equivalent time to consider how their character(s) feels about some of the other characters.

2 Ask the central character(s) to sit in the hot-seat and then ask each of the pairs or groups in turn to state how they feel about the central character(s). Follow this by asking the central character(s) how they feel about the minor character and supplement this by asking the class for their opinion on this relationship. Continue until the class has had an opportunity to explore how each of the minor characters relates to the central character(s).

Option B: Creating groups who would have an opinion about the central character(s)

1 Allow the class some time in pairs or small groups to decide what they might know about the central character(s) and how they feel about them.

2 Then allow the class time to devise questions for the central character(s) from the perspective of their given role. The pupil(s) who will play the central character(s) can use the same time to anticipate what questions they could be asked and prepare for the answers.

3 Make it clear that you will take on the role of chairperson for this process.

VARIATION 3: Half the class hot-seat the other half

Preparation

1 Select one or two large groups of people who would have some information about, or interest in, a central character or narrative event. This might include villagers or residents in a particular area, town councillors, neighbours, peer groups, colleagues, teachers, the police, social workers, historians or private investigators, servants in a large house or the staff of an institution.

2 Arrange the chairs so that one half can see the other half of the class. This can usually be accommodated in classrooms by asking pupils to turn chairs round rather than moving other furniture.

Introduction

1 Draw an imaginary line to split the class into two halves. Explain that one half of the class will take on the roles of reporters or people seeking information, and the other half will take on the chosen role(s) as discussed above. Explain that the reporters will hot-seat the other half as a whole group. It is usually best to restrict the roles to no more than three separate groups.

2 If the reporters are to hot-seat more than one group, then make it clear whether the groups are allowed to respond to each other's answers or not.

3 Make it clear that you will take on the role of chairperson for this process.

4 Before starting the hot-seating, allow the reporters time to work in pairs to prepare what they will ask, and allow the group time in pairs to invent and decide what information they possess about the character or event under interrogation. This should take no more than a few minutes.

Year 7   Skellig

A Literacy Lesson

Main focus: The perspectives of the characters revealed in Chapter 27 of *Skellig*

Link to specific text   *Skellig* by David Almond

Links to the English Framework Objectives for Year 7

Drama:

S&L 15   develop drama techniques to explore in role a variety of situations and texts or respond to stimuli

S&L 17   extend their spoken repertoire by experimenting with language in different roles and dramatic contexts

Reading for meaning:

TLR 6   adopt active reading approaches to engage with and make sense of texts . . .

Persuade, argue, advise:

TLW 17   write informal advice, anticipating the needs, interests and views of the intended reader.

Preparation

1   This lesson works best when the pupils have read the novel up to and including Chapter 27.

2   Organise pupils into pairs and ensure that all pupils have access to Chapter 27 of the novel.

3   Plan how to re-arrange the seating so that half the class can see the other half.

4   You will need the use of a flipchart or white board and will also need to provide rough paper and writing materials for all pupils.

Introduction

1   Share the objectives with the class in relation to the novel.

2   Access prior learning by allowing pairs a few minutes to think of between one and three problems facing Michael at the end of Chapter 26.

3   Read, or re-read, Chapter 27 with the class and point out that the focus of the lesson will be on the relationship between Michael and his friends.

4   Use the flipchart or a white board to quickly wordstorm the problems that Michael has with his friends and the problems his friends have with Michael.

Development

1   Define the writing task by explaining that the class will eventually be asked to write letters to Michael's friends, to help them deal with the problems outlined in the wordstorm.

2   Draw an imaginary line separating the class into two halves and ask the pupils to move their chairs so that one half can see the other half. Explain that one half will be hot-seated as pupils who go to Michael's school, and the other half will ask them questions. Make it clear that the pupils in the hot-seat will know Michael and his friends and have an opinion about them.

3   Allow a few minutes paired work for the pupils playing the school friends to invent what they know about Michael and his friends, and for the others to design a few appropriate questions. The questions should include those that are most likely to reveal information that will be useful to the writing task. Some groups may need examples of these or you may want to devise the first few questions as a whole class and allocate them to individuals to start off the hot-seating.

4   Explain that you will take on the role of chairperson during the hot-seating but you may also ask a few questions yourself or ask those in the hot-seat to elaborate on their answers.

5   Start and stop the hot-seating using clear signals or words such as *ACTION* and *FREEZE*. Keep the hot-seating efficient. Stop once the class has a basic level of information from which to write. You can always start it again if the class does not appear to have taken the information on board.

6 Return to the wordstorming information and ask the class if they have anything to add or omit as a result of the hot-seating.

7 Ask the class to use the information on the wordstorming sheet to help them write between three and five bullet points of things they would like to say to Michael's friends to help them understand what is happening to Michael. Allow pairs to discuss this. Provide an extension task to include three points of advice on how his friends might change their behaviour to help Michael.

8 Take some brief feedback on the bullet points and give the pupils an opportunity to adapt their own points in the light of the feedback from others.

9 Discuss how pupils might convert their bullet points into a draft letter to Michael's friends, to help them understand Michael's behaviour and advise his friends on how best to help him. Use this as an opportunity to discuss the need to consider the likely response of the reader when composing a letter. Link this to the stated objective **TLW 17**. Suggest that they work in pairs to discuss the best order for the bullet points and how to express them before starting to write them in letter form. Decide whether pupils should then write their own letters or write in pairs.

Plenary

1 Stop after a few minutes and ask a few pupils to read out their first lines. Use this to reinforce the message about considering the needs and views of the intended readers.

2 Remind the pupils of the lesson objectives in relation to the work and either ask the class to complete the first draft of their letters for homework or in a subsequent lesson.

Year 8 Holes

A Literacy Lesson

Main focus: Exploring the character of Stanley from the perspective of other characters, using evidence from the text up to the end of Chapter 32

Link to specific text *Holes* by Louis Sachar

Links to the English Framework Objectives for Year 8

Drama:
S&L 15 explore and develop ideas, issues and relationships through work in role
Persuade, argue, advise:
TLW 15 give written advice which offers alternatives and takes account of the possible consequences.

Preparation

1 Place a chair in a central place in the room where every pupil can see it.

2 Select a confident pupil or pair of pupils to represent Stanley in the hot-seating and organise the other pupils into pairs or threes.

3 Make a list of all the characters who live in or near Camp Green Lake and share out the characters so that each pair of pupils is assigned one of the characters. Pupils may be allocated a character each if the class is very small.

4 Provide all pupils with access to the text, rough paper and writing materials.

5 You will need a flipchart or white board.

Introduction

1 Share the lesson objectives with the class in relation to this novel.

2 Access prior learning: organise the class into pairs and present them with a one-minute memory challenge to write a list of all the characters who live in or near Camp Green Lake. Then, write your own list on the board and allow them time to compare your version with theirs.

3 Give out copies of the text and read, or re-read, Chapter 32 to the class.

4 Explain that the pupils will eventually be asked to take on the roles of their allocated characters and write a letter to Stanley. The letter should present the options open to him after the events of Chapter 32 and offer advice from the perspective of their character. Inform the pupils that they will be using a form of hot-seating to help them gain information about how their character might feel about Stanley and his disappearance from the camp. Explain that both the class and the pupil playing Stanley will be asked to comment on how Stanley feels about each of the characters.

Development

1 Give out copies of the text. Ask the pupil or pair of pupils representing Stanley to sit in the hot-seat(s) with a copy of the text. Ask the pupil(s) to consider and make rough notes about how Stanley would feel about each character after he has run away. Encourage the pupil(s) to use the text as a reference and re-assure them that they will be given support from the class during the hot-seating.

2 Ask the other pupils to work in pairs to consider how their character feels about Stanley and his escape. They should record these considerations in bullet points on rough paper. Also encourage them to use the text as a reference.

3 Go through each of the characters in turn and ask the pairs of pupils representing that character to indicate how they feel about Stanley and his escape. They should express this in the first person as if in role. Then ask the class to indicate how Stanley might feel about that character and ask the pupil(s) playing Stanley to express a view in role.

4 Use the word *ACTION* to start the hot-seating and the word *FREEZE* when you want to stop.

5 Take on the role of chairperson in this process by asking the questions in the first person, for example:

Zero, how do you feel about Stanley's escape?

Stanley, how do you feel about Zero as you escape from the camp?

The writing task

Ask the pupils to use the information from the hot-seating to help them draft a letter to Stanley in role as their allotted character. They should give a balanced view of the alternative courses of action facing Stanley and the possible consequences. Then they should give the advice that they feel their character would give to Stanley at the end of Chapter 32, if they were aware of what had happened and were able to contact him. Some groups may need a class discussion to consider what options could be available to Stanley and their likely consequences.

Ask the pupil(s) who played Stanley to select another character in order to complete the above writing task.

Plenary

1 Invite a few pupils to read out the first lines of their letters and use this as an opportunity to point out good practice.

2 Link the work to the lesson objectives and allow the pupils to complete a final version of their letters for homework or in a subsequent lesson.

Year 9   Twelfth Night

A Literacy Lesson

Main focus: to explore the change of mood in *Twelfth Night* after Malvolio's imprisonment, through exploring the response of the other characters

Link to specific text   *Twelfth Night* by William Shakespeare

Links to the English Framework Objectives for Year 9

Drama:

S&L 12   use a range of drama techniques, including work in role, to explore issues, ideas and meanings . . .

S&L 13   develop and compare different interpretations of scenes or plays by Shakespeare or other dramatists.

Preparation

1   Place a chair in a central place in the room where every pupil can see it.

2   Select a confident pupil, or pair of pupils, to represent Malvolio in the hot-seating and organise the other pupils into pairs or threes.

3   Make a list of all the characters who know about Malvolio's imprisonment and share out the characters so that each pair of pupils is assigned to one of the characters. Pupils may be allocated a character each if the class is very small.

4   Provide all pupils with access to a copy of the play, rough paper and writing materials.

5   You will need a flipchart or a white board.

6   Give out copies of the play and read, or re-read, Act 4 Scene 2.

7   Present the pairs or threes with a one-minute memory challenge to write a list of all the characters who are aware of Malvolio's imprisonment after Act 4 Scene 2. Then write your version of the character list on the board and allow them time to compare your version with theirs.

8   Allocate one of the characters to each pair or small group of pupils. In most classes, some pupils will have the same character. Explain that they will eventually be asked to take on the role of their character as a group.

9   Inform the class that they will be using a form of hot-seating to help them gain information about how their character might feel about Malvolio. Make it clear that in this form of hot-seating, each character will be asked to state how they feel about Malvolio's imprisonment. Explain that both the class and the pupil(s) playing Malvolio will be then be asked to comment on how Malvolio feels about each of the characters.

Development

1   Ask the pupil(s) representing Malvolio to sit in the hot-seat with a copy of the play. Ask the pupil(s) to consider and make rough notes on how Malvolio would feel about each character whilst he is imprisoned. Encourage the pupil(s) to use the text as a reference. Re-assure them that they will be given support from the rest of the class.

2   Ask the other pupils to work in pairs to consider how their character feels about Malvolio's imprisonment. They should record these considerations in bullet points on rough paper. Also encourage them to use the text as a reference.

3   Go through each of the characters in turn and ask the pairs of pupils representing that character to indicate how they feel about Malvolio's imprisonment. They should express this in the first person as if in role. Then ask the class to indicate how Malvolio might feel about that character and ask the pupil(s) playing Malvolio to express a view in role.

4   Use the word *ACTION* to start the hot-seating and the word *FREEZE* when you want to stop.

5   Take on the role of chairperson in this process by asking the questions in the first person, for example:
Olivia, how do you feel about Malvolio's imprisonment?
Malvolio, how do you feel about Olivia as you sit in this prison?

Plenary

1   Remind the class of the lesson objectives and relate these to the content of this lesson.

2   Ask one pupil from each group to stand at the front to represent each of the characters who were aware of Malvolio's imprisonment. Then ask the class to arrange them in order of who was most sympathetic and who was least sympathetic to Malvolio's predicament.

3   Refer to the change of mood in the play at this point and discuss how a director might set Act 4 Scene 2 in order to reflect this change of mood. This has the potential to become the introduction to a subsequent lesson based on the direction of this scene.

UNIT SIX SPOTLIGHTING

Making Links

Links to the National Curriculum Key Stages 3 and 4 English Programmes of Study

Drama: **S&L 4**   To participate in a range of drama activities and to evaluate their own and others' contributions, pupils should be taught to:

a) use a variety of dramatic techniques to explore ideas, issues, texts and meanings
b) use different ways to convey action, character, atmosphere and tension when they are scripting and performing plays . . .
c) evaluate critically performances of dramas that they have watched or in which they have taken part.

Breadth of study
Drama activities 11
The range should include:

a) improvisation and working in role
b) devising, scripting and performing plays
c) discussing and reviewing their own and others' performances.

Links to the English Framework Objectives

Year 7
Drama: **S&L 15**
Inform, explain, describe: **TLW 14**

Year 8
Drama: **S&L 16**
Study of literary texts: **TLR 13**

Year 9
Drama: **S&L 12, 14**

Links to Schemes of Work:

Developing writing – setting and character; study of a main character in a novel, narrative poem or play

Links to specific texts

Year 7   Extracts from *The Hobbit* by J.R.R. Tolkien; *Holes* by Louis Sachar; *The Village Dinosaur* by Phyllis Arkle; *Playing on the Edge* by Neil Arksey
Year 8   *About Face* by Paul Whitfield
Year 9   *The Terrible Fate of Humpty Dumpty* by David Calcutt

Definition and Overview

Spotlighting to explore a text through improvised drama or writing and performing scripts

When the teacher shines an imaginary spotlight on a small group of pupils, they perform improvised or scripted snippets of conversation about a character or an event in a narrative text. Pupils usually take on large group roles connected to the narrative, such as neighbours, eye-witnesses or other groups with a vested interest in the events. If such roles do not exist in the text already, they can be created specifically for the spotlighting exercise.

Spotlighting to create a character for a drama or for narrative writing

As an imaginary character walks down a street, the pupils roleplay the people in the houses. These people are spotlighted to perform conversations that reveal their opinions of that character. Pupils then incorporate this character into a subsequent drama or into their individual story writing.

Spotlighting to create a setting for a drama or for narrative writing

Pupils are arranged in groups around the room. An imaginary character walks along a vaguely defined route, such as by the sea or up a hill to an extinct volcano. The imaginary route is represented by a set route around the room, which passes by every group of pupils. As the character walks along the route they stop beside each group of pupils along the way. Each group of pupils puts the spotlight on their part of the route by describing what the character sees, hears or senses at that particular point. They may also indicate the character's response. This informs the context for a subsequent drama or the setting for a story.

Teaching and Learning Rationale

Spotlighting:

- ensures that all pupils make a significant contribution to the lesson
- creates an ethos of respect for pupils' ideas
- represents an imaginative way of assessing pupils' response to a text
- can bring a challenging narrative to life
- has the potential to create a deeper understanding of characters and events in texts
- supports the writing of short scenes, character studies and settings
- enables all the pupils to engage in a dramatic performance within a short space of time
- encourages pupils to produce a short piece of work which allows time to work on quality
- develops speaking and listening skills through collaborative group work and discussion
- can easily be recorded onto an audio cassette to produce a radio play or a secret tape
- can take place in a classroom setting or in a drama studio.

Year 7   Story Settings

A Literacy Lesson

Main focus: Creating a setting for a story

Links to specific texts   *The Hobbit* by J.R.R. Tolkien (page 1); *Holes* by Louis Sachar (page 3); *The Village Dinosaur* by Phyllis Arkle (page 7); *Playing on the Edge* by Neil Arksey (page 5)

Links to the English Framework Objectives for Year 7

Drama:
S&L 15   develop drama techniques to explore in role a variety of situations and texts or respond to stimuli

Inform, explain, describe:
TLW 14   describe an object, person or setting in a way that includes relevant details and is accurate and evocative.

Preparation

1 Select a suitable broad setting for a story with potential for a character to walk or travel through, for example, the seashore, a street, a derelict building, a path to an extinct volcano, the woods, a new house, a new school, a deserted village, a desert island, another planet or a place in a defined historical period.

2 Organise pupils into pairs or threes and plan a route round the room that will pass by or near every group.

3 Decide on a genre for the story and then create a suitable type of character without providing too many details, for example, a horror story with an old person in a shabby coat, a detective story with a young woman wearing expensive clothes or an adventure story with a child carrying a hold-all.

4 Make one copy of photocopiable sheets 6.1a, 6.1b, 6.1c and 6.1d.

5 Provide pupils with one copy of photocopiable sheet 6.2 per group and some rough paper and writing materials. You will need white boards if you run a guided writing group (see the differentiation section in the writing task).

Introduction

1 Share the lesson objectives with the class.

2 Make links between reading and writing. Read some of the extracts from photocopiable sheets 6.1a, 6.1b, 6.1c and 6.1d as examples of how settings can be organised in books, e.g. starting with a description of a setting as in *Holes* and *The Hobbit*, or including a description of a setting alongside the actions of a character as in *The Village Dinosaur* and *Playing on the Edge*.

3 Inform the pupils that by the end of this lesson they will have written part of a story that describes a setting alongside the actions of a character. Inform the class of the genre of the story and the kind of setting and character that will form the basis of their writing.

4 Ask pupils to suggest aspects of the setting that the writer might focus on, for example: dark places for a horror story, and unusual buildings and exotic scenes for an adventure story abroad. Then allow pupils 2 minutes in pairs to decide on between one and three aspects of their own.

5 Take feedback from a few pairs and ask the class to comment on the appropriateness of each suggestion in terms of the kind of story intended.

Development

1 Organise the pupils into their groups and explain that a route around the room will represent the route taken by a character in the story. Then describe the route around the room and explain the following process: one person will take on the role of a character for the purposes of the forthcoming spotlighting exercise. The character will walk along the route and as they do so they will stop beside each group of pupils along the way. Each group of pupils will be put under an imaginary spotlight to describe what the character sees, hears or senses at that particular point. They should also indicate the character's response. Make it clear that when the character moves on, the spotlight moves with them to the next group.

2 Allow the groups about 5 minutes to complete photocopiable sheet 6.2. Inform the class that they are to incorporate the information on the sheet into what they will say when under the spotlight. Stop the above activity mid-flow to allow one or two pupils to feedback on ideas so far, and then remind them that, if they have not already done so, they should now move on from the sketch to the senses and emotions.

3 When some pupils have completed the sheet, stop the activity and remind all groups that they should now begin to compose what they will say when under the spotlight. If necessary, use one of the groups' sheets to provide an example of what this might sound like before the pupils recommence the task.

4 Also ask them to decide how they will present their information in the spotlight, for example: chorally, shared out in sections or through one spokesperson.

5 Set up the spotlighting by reminding the class of how it will proceed. Remind groups to be silent when they are not in the spotlight. Emphasise the need to listen to each group in order to incorporate the ideas into their stories. Start and stop the process through the words *ACTION* and

FREEZE and set the tone by introducing the story as narrative: e.g. As the old person walked along the seashore this is what they saw'.

If pupils speak out of turn or struggle to respond then temporarily stop the action to deal with the problem.

The writing task

1 After the spotlighting, allow the class 1 minute to write down three parts of the setting that they think they may incorporate into their own stories. They should complete this task as individuals but should be allowed to discuss their ideas with their group if they wish.

2 Now allow the pupils 2 minutes to write a first draft of the first few sentences of their story, which starts with the character walking along the route used in the spotlighting.

3 Stop the activity on time and ask some pupils to read out their first drafts. Use this as an opportunity to point out good practice and ask the class to give advice on how these first drafts could be improved.

4 Ask pupils to complete a draft and then a final version of the first paragraph of their story, which deals with the route taken by the character.

Differentiation

If most of the class need support with the above task, it is best to carry it out as a shared writing activity, making one story opening from the pupils' suggestions. If less than seven pupils need extra support with the above task, then work with them as a small guided writing group, whilst the others complete the task as individuals. Support this guided writing group by sharing ideas and asking the pupils to write their story openings, one sentence at a time on white boards. Stop the group at various points and ask them to read out their work to the others. The group will then consider each contribution and offer advice on how to improve them. Extend the task by challenging more confident writers to write a setting based on the spotlighting but without the character.

Plenary

1 Remind the pupils of the lesson objectives and link to the content of the lesson.

2 Ask pupils to work in pairs for 1 minute to record between one and three things they will remember about the work in this lesson. Take brief feedback.

3 Ask pupils to extend the story for homework by writing an outline of the plot (optional).

Year 8   Illness in the Family

A Literacy Lesson

Main focus: Exploring issues about family illness in *About Face*

Links to specific texts   *About Face* by Paul Whitfield; *Harry Pushed Her* by Peter Thabit Jones

Links to the English Framework Objectives for Year 8

Drama:

S&L 16   collaborate in, and evaluate, the presentation of dramatic performances, scripted and unscripted, which explore character, relationships and issues

Study of literary texts:

TLR 13   read a substantial text (novel, play or work of one poet) revising and refining interpretations of subject matter, style and technique.

Preparation

1 Pupils should have sufficient copies of the extract on photocopiable sheet 6.3, which is the opening of the play. In this extract, Rachel, the central character is tormented by her school friends for being a loner and having a *strange* mother.

2 Organise the room so that pupils can work in seven small groups. Also, plan a route around the room that passes near each of the groups.

3 Make sufficient copies of photocopiable sheet 6.4 (for optional link to drama lesson).

Introduction

1 Share the lesson objectives with the class.

2 Organise the class into seven small groups (made up of boys and girls if possible).

3 Hand out the extract and allocate each group to one of the following characters:
Samantha, Emma, Bill, Hayley, Joe, Amy, Dean. Then allocate one pupil from each group to read the part of their character when you read the extract of the playscript.

4 Read the extract through twice; once with the pupils sitting in their desks and again with pupils standing at the front as if performing it. Select someone to represent Rachel for the second reading.

Development

1 Explain that you will be asking each group to create an extra scene following on from this extract. The scene will involve each of Rachel's friends talking about Rachel to their other friends during the school lunch break. Dean's group will devise a scene in which Dean talks to his other friends about Rachel. And Amy's group will devise a scene where Amy talks to her other friends about Rachel, and so on. The scene should be a polished improvisation involving everyone in the group and should last about 1 minute. The pupils who played one of the characters in the class play-reading should play the same character in their improvisations.

2 Make it clear that the improvised conversation should include speculations about what could be wrong with Rachel's mother. Talk about what could be wrong with her and establish the fact that the friends in the play do not appear to know very much about it and are left to speculate and make assumptions. Remind groups to look in the extract for clues about how their main character might think and behave.

3 Before groups begin their task, establish some ground rules about acceptable behaviour during improvisations. These might include the following:
   a) pupils should not use bad language or say anything that might be offensive to any individual or group.
   b) for safety reasons, pupils should avoid any physical contact during the improvisation.

4 Give pupils a set time of about 10 to 15 minutes to plan and rehearse an improvisation.

5 Visit each group to ensure that they will have something to present to the class during the spotlighting activity.

Differentiation

Support less confident groups by suggesting that characters speak just one line each and speak in turn. You may also suggest a few opening lines, such as: *Rachel's on her own again, have you heard about her mum?*

Encourage more confident groups to consider the use of silences to create tension and the use of contrast to maintain the attention of the audience.

Final rehearsal

When every group has prepared at least a few lines of conversation, stop the activity. Explain that, when you say the word *ACTION,* all groups should hold a final rehearsal simultaneously, to a set time of between 1 and 1½ minutes. If groups finish before time they should wait in silence. Warn the class that every group should stop after the allotted time. Use the word *FREEZE* to indicate that time is up.

Final spotlighting

Explain that you will walk around the class and point to each group as if you were shining an imaginary spotlight on them. When the spotlight is on a group, they should perform their improvisations but when the spotlight moves away they should stop. Make it clear that groups should stop even if they have more to say, as this technique requires snippets of conversation to be overheard. Set the scene by asking the class to imagine that these are conversations around the school at lunchtime.

When everyone is clear about the process, orchestrate the improvisations by walking around the room, pointing to groups as if they are in a spotlight. Ensure that you stay with each group for no longer than 1 minute.

Evaluations

After the spotlighting, allow groups 1 minute to think of between one and three things they thought worked well in their performance. Some groups may need suggestions as to what things to consider, for example: clarity of expression, use of pauses, the way the conversation flowed naturally, the use of humour or the believable way the characters related to each other.

Ask the class for their response to the information gleaned from the spotlighting in relation to the issues that may emerge in the play. For example, they may want to discuss how people feel when they have relatives who are unusual in some way or why Rachel may not have told her friends about her mother.

Plenary

1 If you intend to read the rest of the play with the class, ask them to speculate on what the next scene could be and promise to read the rest of the play in subsequent lessons.
2 Link the work to the stated lesson objectives.

Link to subsequent Writing Lessons

Ask groups to adapt and convert their improvisations into scripts, using the same layout as the play. They can then either record their script readings onto an audio tape or perform them live as an imaginary radio play.

Link to subsequent Drama Lesson

1 Give each pupil a copy of the poem *Harry Pushed Her* by Peter Thabit Jones, on photocopiable sheet 6.4, and read it through to the pupils twice.
2 Discuss links between Harry in this poem and Rachel in the play *About Face*.
3 Ask pupils to work in groups to create and present a freeze-frame with thought tracking to represent this poem.

Year 9   Bullying

A Literacy Lesson

Main focus:
a) exploring issues of bullying in *The Terrible Fate of Humpty Dumpty* by David Calcutt
b) writing scripts based on improvisations.

 Links to specific text   *The Terrible Fate of Humpty Dumpty* by David Calcutt

 **Links to the English Framework Objectives for Year 9**

Drama:

S&L 12   use a range of drama techniques, including work in role, to explore issues, ideas and meanings e.g. by playing out hypotheses, by changing perspectives

S&L 14   convey action, character, atmosphere and tension when scripting and performing plays.

Preparation

1 Whilst this lesson is designed to take place after pupils have already read the play, pupils should have sufficient copies of the play to refer to.
2 Organise the room so that pupils can work in small groups of three to four pupils.
3 Plan a route around the room that passes near each of the groups.

Introduction

1 Share the lesson objectives with the class.
2 Ask the class to imagine a new scene in the play which takes place just after Terry's funeral. The scene involves the pupils from Terry's school making comments about the events that led up to Terry's death and includes their opinions on the gang members and other people involved.
3 Ask the class to play the parts of the pupils. Explain that they will be asked to improvise their conversations in groups before writing the new scene.
4 Organise the pupils into their groups and allow them a few minutes to discuss what the characters may know about the gang members and the kind of opinions they may have about the whole situation. Encourage them to select opinions that would make a good scene in the play. Discuss a few examples with the whole group beforehand if necessary.

Development

1 Discuss ideas for opening lines, such as *This never should have happened / Someone should have told the teachers* or *He was a loner so what do you expect?* Then allow groups 1 minute to decide on their opening line and who will say it.
2 Use the word ACTION as a signal for each group to start their spontaneous improvisation as the school pupils who talk in groups after Terry's funeral. Warn them that, after a few minutes, you will stop the improvisations using the word *FREEZE.*
3 Stop the improvisations and explain that you will now bring each group to life again in turn, as if you were turning a spotlight on them to perform. Groups should not be asked to move to the front to perform. Now allow groups a few minutes to select a suitable part of their improvisation to re-run for the spotlighting. Allow each group about 30 seconds to perform a snippet of their conversation.
4 Discuss the effect that these conversations might have if put together as an extra scene in the play. Talk about which group's conversation would be best first and which last. Also, discuss any other points about the order and how the whole thing might be performed to make it consistent with the rest of the play.

Writing task

Ask each group to work together to script part of their improvisation as a 30 second snippet of conversation in the style of the rest of the play. Suggest that pupils take turns to be group scribe. Explain that these snippets will eventually be put together to create a new scene. Encourage groups to build in characterisation and tension when turning their improvised work into script. Discuss some examples beforehand if necessary, for example, one pupil might reveal that they helped Stubbs or perhaps one of the group may admit to being bullied by Stubbs themselves. Also discuss the power of using pauses before and after important pieces of information or using silences to make a moment more tense. Some groups may also consider using contrasts of funny comments interspersed with serious ones.

Plenary

1 Ask each group to read out their scripts so far and discuss how they might be linked together to form a scene.
2 Link the work to the stated lesson objectives.

Link to subsequent lesson

When pupils have completed their scripts, work as a class to agree any stage directions and decide on where this new scene might best be placed within the existing play. Then put the whole thing together as a new scene, which can finally be read into a cassette player or read out in class as an imaginary radio play. The final work will be enhanced if the scene can be word-processed.

UNIT SEVEN   WRITING PLAYS

Making Links

Links to the National Curriculum Key Stages 3 and 4 English Programmes of Study

Drama: **S&L 4**   To participate in a range of drama activities and to evaluate their own work and others' contributions, pupils should be taught to . . .

b) use different ways to convey action, character, atmosphere and tension when they are scripting and performing plays

c) appreciate how the structure and organisation of scenes and plays contribute to dramatic effect

d) evaluate critically performances of dramas that they have watched or in which they have taken part.

Breadth of Study

Drama Activities 11

The range should include:

b) devising, scripting and performing in plays

c) discussing and reviewing their own and others' performances.

Links to the English Framework Objectives

Year 7

Drama: **S&L 16**

Year 8

Drama: **S&L 16**

Year 9

Drama: **S&L 14**

Standard English and language variation: **Sn 11**

Links to Schemes of Work

Reading and writing playscripts

Links to specific texts

Year 9   *The Canterbury Tales* by Geraldine McCaughrean;

Year 9   *Chaucer The Canterbury Tales* trans. by Nevill Coghill;

Year 9   *Chaucer The Pardoner's Prologue and Tale* by Geoffrey Chaucer;

Year 9   *Dicing with Death* by Simon Adorian

Overview of Ways to Introduce Play Writing

The five methods outlined here need to be supplemented with provision for pupils to read, act and watch a range of plays as models for their own writing.

1. Convert a section of a familiar story into a script:

Pupils write a simple script to represent all or part of a traditional or well-known story e.g. a fairy tale, myth or legend.

Teaching and learning rationale

This helps inexperienced play writers to focus on the features of play writing by taking away the need to compose a new plotline (see photocopiable sheet 7.1 for a *Checklist for Writing Plays*)

2. Convert a piece of prose into a script:

A section of a narrative text is re-written as a play. Pupils highlight all the dialogue in a piece of narrative text and re-write it as the dialogue in a play script. This can also be achieved using a computer. They then add other relevant information such as stage directions through a narrator or chorus. Use plays that have been adapted from novels, such as the play version of *Bill's New Frock* by Anne Fine as models.

Teaching and learning rationale

Pupils learn to identify the essential differences between a narrative expressed as prose or poem, and a script, by becoming involved in the process of turning prose into play. The process also helps pupils to see the need for stage directions to supplement the dialogue in a play and illustrates the function of a narrator or a chorus.

3. Convert an improvisation into script:

Pupils improvise scenes in groups and then adapt these to make a scripted version.

Teaching and learning rationale

This method allows pupils some ownership over the content of the script and helps to motivate pupils to write. It also illustrates the difference between improvisation and script by emphasising a need to set stage directions in a script so that others know how to perform the piece.

4. Write additional scenes for existing plays:

Pupils create an additional scene within a set play, without contradicting the existing plotline. For example, pupils write an additional scene in Shakespeare's *Macbeth* where the servants talk about the murder of Duncan. These scenes are often comments on the action by minor characters or groups who witness the events, such as servants, neighbours, school pupils or colleagues. (See Unit 6: Spotlighting Year 9 example on p. 62 for an additional scene in the play *The Terrible Fate of Humpty Dumpty* by David Calcutt.)

Teaching and learning rationale

Pupils can use the existing play as a guide to the content and style required in their own work. This encourages the pupils to make the important link between reading a play and writing a play.

5. Write short plays for a purpose:

Pupils write short 1 or 2 minute plays, to be performed either as radio plays that can be recorded onto an audio cassette tape, or read out to the class. Groups may also be asked to write plays for other groups to perform, or contribute to a book of short class plays to be read and/or performed by other members of the class.

Teaching and learning rationale

To write plays as a form without a purpose can appear meaningless to many pupils. They are more likely to be motivated to write plays if they know that the plays will eventually be performed. Many pupils enjoy performing their own plays, but the necessity for stage directions becomes more apparent if the play is written for another group to perform.

Several short plays lasting 1 to 2 minutes can be performed within one lesson. These can be written and performed as radio plays to be recorded onto an audio cassette tape, or read aloud to the class, thus avoiding the need to learn lines by heart. Writing short plays also ensures that pupils have time to focus on quality rather than quantity. Time can be spent on developing characters beyond the stereotypical and using dialogue to define relationships and create a sense of time and place. Short plays also allow time for pupils to include features such as descriptions about the set and lighting, sound effects, instructions on how actors should say their lines and appropriate stage directions.

Year 7   The Bradley Painting Challenge

Two Literacy Lessons

Main focus: Writing for a purpose: recording playscripts onto an audio cassette tape

 Links to the English Framework Objectives for Year 7

Drama:
S&L 16   work collaboratively to devise and present scripted and unscripted pieces, which maintain the attention of the audience.

Lesson 1

Preparation

1   You will need a flipchart or white board. Pupils will need rough paper and writing materials.
2   Organise the class into groups with about three pupils in each group.
3   Make one copy per group of photocopiable sheets 7.1 (*Checklist for Writing Plays)* and 7.2.

Introduction

1   Share the lesson objective with the class.
2   Organise the class to sit in their groups and hand each group a copy of the paintings on photocopiable sheet 7.2.
3   Ask the class to imagine the following situation:
    The paintings on the sheet are the winners of a local competition known as The Bradley Painting Challenge. The competition was open to local artists living in the small town of Bradley. The public have been invited to view the work of the three winners at the Bradley Art Gallery.
    Following an attempted burglary the previous week, Bradley Art Gallery installed CCTV in every room. This also picked up the voices of the visitors as they talked about the winning paintings.
4   Explain that the class will be asked to devise, script and record the visitors' conversations about the three winning paintings, in order to create the Art Gallery audio tape on the day of the public viewing. Make it clear that the visitors were unaware of the CCTV.
5   Explain that when the owners of the Art Gallery heard the tape they discovered the following things:
    a) most people viewed the paintings in groups of two or three
    b) people often disagreed with each other about the paintings
    c) some people disagreed with the judges' decision for first prize
    d) many knew the artists personally and some visitors had strong opinions about these people.
6   Write the above findings on the flipchart or white board and ask groups to include some of these aspects in their scripts.

Development

1   Make it clear that pupils should write one draft script per group.
2   Inform the class that each conversation should last approximately 30 seconds to 1 minute and should include a speaking part for everyone in the group. Encourage groups to make their conversations realistic and interesting by including comments about the artists and/or disagreements about the paintings. Discuss other possibilities such as including amusing anecdotes or comments, quarrelling children or references to other art exhibitions in the gallery. Discuss a few ideas on what visitors might say about the paintings.

3 Allow groups about 5 to 10 minutes to make a rough draft of their conversation. Ask groups to start by deciding on one character for each person in the group. Make it clear that these should be imaginary people visiting the Art Gallery and not themselves. Remind pupils how to set out a script so that it is clear when each person is speaking and hand out copies of the *Checklist for Writing Plays* on photocopiable sheet 7.1.

4 Visit each group to check for content. Then stop the activity and ask groups to focus on making their first and last lines indicate that the people are arriving and leaving the room. Discuss some possibilities before asking groups to resume their work e.g. 'These must be the paintings over here' . . . 'I'm tired of this. Can we go for a cup of tea?'

5 As groups complete their drafts, ask them to read their scripts aloud and time themselves to see if they need to adjust their work to fit the allotted time of between 30 seconds and 1 minute. Groups can time each other if appropriate. Groups who work slowly and do not have time to do this should estimate the length of their work by comparing the length of their script with others.

Plenary

1 Ask a few groups to read out the start of their scripts and use this as an opportunity to point out good practice.

2 Collect in the draft copies. Pupils should receive your written comments next lesson.

Lesson 2

Preparation

1 Comment on appropriate content and the quality of the first and last lines in the scripts.

2 Photocopy these final scripts for those pupils who do not have their own copies (approx two thirds of the class).

3 Obtain an audio cassette player (a simple one with a built-in microphone will suffice) to record the pupils reading their scripts.

4 Define an area of the room suitable for pupils to record their scripts onto the cassette player. This area should be visible to the rest of the class. Three chairs should be arranged so that pupils can sit near the machine with their backs to the class.

Introduction

1 Remind pupils of the lesson objective and the task from last lesson.

2 Return the scripts to the groups and hand out the photocopies so that each pupil has a draft copy of their group script. Then allow the groups a few minutes to re-read the scripts and make amendments.

Development

1 Explain that because these scripts will be recorded on a tape, pupils will be unable to use facial expressions or body movements to make their words more interesting and so they must rely on reading with expression.

2 Ask the class to suggest some feelings that might be appropriate for the characters in this situation and write these on the board. Add some of your own if necessary, such as: bored, impatient, curious, pleased, surprised, tired and angry. Then take a line from one of the scripts and read it in a number of different ways to indicate some of the feelings on the board. Ask the class to guess the feeling each time. Point out that people's feelings can affect the way they say their words. Explain that script writers can indicate how a character speaks a line by putting the description in brackets within the character's line, for example:

TOM (*Abruptly*)   What is it?

3 Allow groups a few minutes to go through their scripts and add between three and five bracketed instructions to indicate how their characters should say their lines. Then take a few examples as feedback.

4   Then allow groups a few more minutes to practise reading their scripts aloud with expression ready for the recordings.

5   Pair groups up to give each an opportunity to read their script aloud to someone else (optional).

6   Before groups are asked to come to the audio cassette player to record their scripts, allow all groups to hold a final rehearsal. Organise this by asking all groups to begin simultaneously when you say *ACTION*. Time the rehearsal and explain that if any group exceeds 1 minute they will be asked to stop.

7   Collect the scripts so that pupils are not tempted to carry on working on them whilst others are recording.

8   Call groups out to the recording area in turn and explain that should anyone make a serious error, you will press the pause button to avoid the need to re-record the whole script. Insist that the class remain silent during each of the 1 minute recordings.

Plenary

● When all groups have recorded their scripts, play the whole tape back to the class and ask them to judge it on whether it sounds realistic and interesting. Make an agreement beforehand that no-one is to cause offence by making personal or negative comments about the way the script is read.

● Remind pupils of the lesson objective and ask them to work in pairs to think of between one and three aspects of script writing that they think they will remember as a result of these two lessons. Take brief feedback and link comments to the lesson objective.

Follow up work

Designate one pupil from each group to copy their script on a word processor. Collect these to make a class script of the secret tape, along with the cassette tape itself.

Year 8   Waiting in the Queue

Two Literacy/Drama Lessons

Main focus: converting improvisation into a script

Links to the English Framework Objectives for Year 8

Drama:

S&L 16   collaborate in, and evaluate, the presentation of dramatic performances, scripted and unscripted, which explore character, relationships and issues.

Lesson 1

Preparation

1   Clear a space in the room for a performance area for a small group of pupils.

2   Organise the class into small groups with about three or four in each group.

3   You will need the use of a flipchart or white board.

Introduction

1   Share the lesson objective with the class.

2   Choose a confident group and ask them to stand in a line in the performance area, facing the class. Ask the class to imagine that these are people who have been standing in a queue for a long time, waiting to take part in a talent competition.

3   Ask the class to suggest a range of different characters and reasons why they might be there. Then discuss how the characters in the queue might be feeling about the waiting and about each other. Encourage a range of possiblities and record these on the board. Now ask each pupil in the queue to quickly decide on a character and then decide how their character might be feeling. Ask the queue to take up positions that indicate how they are feeling and ask the class to guess what their

feelings are. Discuss how you might indicate these feelings on paper, if you were writing a play that starts with this image of a queue. Use this experience to discuss stage directions and instructions on how actors should position themselves on stage.

Development

1 Ask the class to work in groups to devise an improvisation based on a queue for some kind of talent contest.

2 Share the following rules with the class:
   - The improvisation should last between 1 and 2 minutes and everyone in the group should have a reasonable speaking part.
   - The work should begin and end with a frozen image, starting with the stationary queue and ending with a particular event or an important statement by one of the characters.
   - The improvisation should bring out tension between the characters as well as other relationships.
   - The improvisation can include contrasts such as amusing moments interspersed with tension.
   - Characters can say anything they like, as long as it does not involve bad language or cause offence.
   - In the interests of safety, violent physical contact between characters and physical stunts should be avoided.

3 Encourage groups to establish their characters and begin to improvise within the first 5 minutes.

4 Support any groups who initially struggle to make decisions or come to an agreement about the characters or the opening scene. It is important that groups keep up with each other in terms of being ready to perform at least the beginning of the improvisation.

5 As groups devise their improvisations, resist the temptation to let them show you everything they have done so far. If there is a problem then ask the group to show you the part causing difficulty, and then work with them to solve it. Once groups have begun to improvise, it may be useful to stop the activity and suggest some contrast to build tension. Use the information in the section on contrast on photocopiable sheet 7.1, *Checklist for Writing Plays*:
   Contrast can be used to build tension:
   a) *moments of silence placed within conversations make scenes more interesting by creating tension between characters*
   b) *pleasant or amusing sections placed between sad or tragic sections of a play make the tragic parts seem even more tragic.*

6 When you are satisfied that all groups can make a reasonable attempt at an improvisation, stop the work and invite all groups to hold a final rehearsal simultaneously.

7 Now let each group perform their improvisation to the rest of the class and ask the class to pick out between one and three aspects that they liked about each performance. Use this as an opportunity to point out good practice.

Plenary

Explain that in the next lesson pupils will work on adapting a small part of their improvisations to form a script. In order to prepare for this, allow groups a few minutes to decide which part of the improvisation to script and consider anything they would like to change. As a guide, the scripted section should involve all the characters in a speaking part and should last about 30 seconds.

Lesson 2

Preparation

1 Pupils will need writing materials.
2 Make copies of photocopiable sheet 7.1, *Checklist for Writing Plays*.

Introduction

Remind pupils of the lesson objective and the forthcoming task to write up part of their improvisations in script form. Make it clear that each member of the group will need to make their own copy of the script.

Development

1   Give pupils copies of photocopiable sheet 7.1, *Checklist for Writing Plays* and discuss the need for stage directions and advice for some actors on how to say their lines.
2   Break up the process by giving groups a few minutes to make a final decision on which part of their improvisation to script and to begin a rough draft of the first few lines. Groups can work on one copy between them but they should be encouraged to take turns to scribe. Then stop the activity and ask some groups to feedback to the class. Use this to point out good practice and make any other relevant teaching points.
3   Now allow groups a further 10 minutes to make a rough draft of their script and begin to edit before making the final copy.

Plenary

1   Allow about 2 minutes for each group to identify and note down between one and three aspects of their script that they think work well and between one and three aspects they would like to improve. Then take brief feedback by asking for one point from each group.
2   Now allow pupils a further minute to work in pairs to identify between one and three aspects of improvisation and script writing that they will remember as a result of these lessons. If pupils need support, then take some suggestions beforehand and record these on the board for pairs to consider.
3   Remind pupils of the lesson objective and link to the work over the two lessons.

Links to further lessons

1   Ask each pupil to improve and/or extend their script as an individual task next lesson or for homework.
2   Collect good copies of the scripts and/or word-process them and present them as a book of scripts for the school library.
3   Invite pupils to read out their scripts to the class for positive evaluation and constructive advice on how to improve them.

Year 9   *Versions of The Pardoner's Tale*

A Literacy Lesson

Main focus: converting prose into a playscript, using four versions/interpretations of Chaucer's *The Pardoner's Tale*

Links with specific texts: *The Canterbury Tales* by Geraldine McCaughrean; *The Canterbury Tales* translated by Nevill Coghill; *The Pardoner's Prologue and Tale* by Geoffrey Chaucer; *Dicing with Death* by Simon Adorian

Links to the English Framework Objectives for Year 9

Drama:
S&L 14   convey action, character, atmosphere and tension when scripting and performing plays
Standard English and language variation:
Sn 11   investigate ways English has changed over time and identify current trends of language change.

Preparation

1   Organise pupils into pairs.
2   Make sufficient copies of photocopiable sheet 7.1, *Checklist for Writing Plays* and the extracts on photocopiable sheets 7.3, 7.4a, 7.4b, 7.4c and 7.5a, 7.5b (one copy per pair of pupils).
3   Pupils will need sheets of lined paper, pencils/pens and highlighters (or coloured pencils to underline different sections of text).

Introduction

1 Share the lesson objectives with the class.
2 Hand out copies of *Death's Murderers* on photocopiable sheet 7.3 and read with the class. Make sure the pupils understand Snatch's misapprehension that Death is a real person.
3 Hand out copies of the two extracts on photocopiable sheets 7.4a, 7.4b and 7.4c and whilst you are reading them through to the class, ask them to think about what these have to do with the first extract. Use this to explain the links between the three extracts in terms of levels of difficulty in English.
4 Allow pairs 1 minute to highlight all the words in the original extract that they do not understand. Take feedback by asking them to identify which of these words they might be able to guess by using the translated extract. Use this to point out the way words have changed over time.

Development

1 Explain that the task for this lesson will be for pupils to work in pairs to convert the prose extract headed *Death's Murderers* into part of a play. Ask the class to scan the extract to identify a list of characters for the play version and then write these on the board for pupils to refer to when writing the play.
2 Before pupils begin the task, ask them to highlight each character's speaking part in different colours on the photocopiable sheet and write the name of the character in the left-hand margin each time. When writing the dialogue as a script, they should write it on every other line, so that they can use the space between the lines for stage directions and instructions for the actors. Ask pupils to include details of the set at the beginning of the play and any suggestions for lighting.
3 Hand out copies of the checklist on photocopiable sheet 7.1 for reference if necessary.
4 Allow pupils about 15 minutes to complete the play in rough with an extension task to carry out a final edit and make a final copy.

Plenary

1 Hand out copies of the extract *Dicing with Death* on photocopiable sheets 7.5a and 7.5b. Allocate pupils to read the parts and the stage directions and so on. Then read the extract as a class and point out that, like them, the playwright has turned the story into a play. Discuss how successful they feel the playwright has been and discuss some of the problems in converting prose into script.
2 Remind the pupils of the lesson objectives and link to the work in this lesson.

Links to further lessons

Allow pairs time to complete the final versions of their scripts and allow them to read these scripts to the class or onto an audio cassette tape. Collect these hand-written versions or make word-processed versions and present these as a book of scripts entitled: *Ways into Chaucer's The Pardoner's Tale.*

UNIT EIGHT   PERFORMANCE AND EVALUATION

Performance – Making Links

Links to the National Curriculum Key Stages 3 and 4 English Programmes of Study

Drama: **S&L 4**   To participate in a range of drama activities and to evaluate their own work and others' contributions, pupils should be taught to . . .

b) use different ways to convey action, character, atmosphere and tension when they are scripting and performing plays

Breadth of Study
Drama activities 11
The range should include:
a) improvisation and working in role
b) devising, scripting and performing in plays
c) discussing and reviewing their own and others' performances.

Links to the English Framework Objectives

Year 7
Drama: **S&L 16**

Year 8
Drama: **S&L 16**

Year 9
Drama: **S&L 14**

Rationale

The strategies in this section are designed to support all Key Stage 3 year groups to achieve the requirements of the National Curriculum in relation to performing plays (EN1 POS 4b) and are applicable to most plays, improvisations and drama scripts. They are also designed to help pupils appreciate the art of presenting a play in terms of effectively communicating ideas and issues to an audience in an entertaining way, rather than just walking the moves and delivering the lines. Strategies should be selected according to the needs of the group and the confines of time and space. However, the list below indicates those strategies which are *particularly* relevant to the English Framework drama objective for each year group.

Year 7

Links to the English Framework Objectives for Year 7

Drama:
S&L 16   work collaboratively to devise and present scripted and unscripted pieces, which maintain the attention of the audience.

Suitable strategies:
- owning the script
- the echo
- line partners
- marking pauses.

Year 8

Links to the English Framework Objectives for Year 8

Drama:

S&L 16   collaborate in, and evaluate, the presentation of dramatic performances, scripted and unscripted, which explore character, relationships and issues.

Suitable strategies:

- the freeze-frame
- the character walkabout
- greetings in role
- hot-seating
- improvising imaginary situations.

Year 9

Links to the English Framework Objectives for Year 9

Drama:

S&L 14   convey action, character, atmosphere and tension when scripting and performing plays.

Suitable strategies:

- marking pauses
- the freeze-frame
- hot-seating
- thought tracking
- the silent movie
- creating atmosphere through set, lighting and costume.

Overview

Strategies to Develop Pupils' Performance Skills

Owning the script

Make photocopies so that every pupil has their own script. Ask pupils to highlight their parts on their individual scripts and write notes in the margin on various points e.g. note the thoughts and feelings of their character at key points in the play.

The echo

Divide the class into two groups and position them at opposite sides of the room with their highlighted scripts as above. Ask each pupil in turn to read out one of their lines clearly and audibly so that the pupils on the other side of the room can hear and understand what is being said. After each pupil has read out their line, the pupils on the opposite side of the room should repeat the line as an echo. If there is a discrepancy, the pupil should attempt to say the line again perhaps a little louder or slower. Advise pupils to say their lines slightly slower than they would in real life, to help the audience hear every word. Encourage pupils to relax and breathe normally but ask them to think about the concept of the need to *share* their lines with the audience.

Encourage pupils to look just above the heads of their audience as they speak their lines or direct their lines to an imaginary member of the audience sitting at the back of the room. Discourage the tendency for pupils to shout out their lines or over-articulate the words. Explain that a booming voice can sometimes obscure the words and become irritating for the audience. Encourage variety in the voice and if appropriate, refer to *Eight Tips for using the Voice on Stage* on photocopiable sheet 8.1 to help pupils with this work.

Allow each pupil a maximum of three attempts to get the echo right, before moving on to the next pupil. Select pupils from different sides of the room each time in order to alternate the echo. This can be adapted for use with longer passages when lines are learnt by heart. In this case the echo is replaced by the pupils across the room raising their hands whenever they cannot hear the lines clearly.

Line partners

Point out to pupils that it is difficult to project the voice and speak with expression when reading from a script. Encourage pupils to learn their lines by heart as early as possible. Organise groups into pairs to help each other learn their lines. Discuss helpful techniques such as learning the cue line as a lead-in, tape recording the lines and reading along with them, underlining key words or walking around the room saying the lines aloud.

Marking pauses

Draw attention to the power of pauses in allowing the audience time to absorb the information and observe the reactions of the other characters to the spoken dialogue. Pauses can also be used to enhance comedy by placing a brief pause just before the amusing key word or phrase and another just after, to allow the audience time to laugh before moving on. Explain the need for all the cast to be aware of pauses in comedy so that everyone knows when to wait for laughs. Pauses can be marked on the script by using one slash for a short pause (/) and a double slash for a longer pause (//).

The freeze-frame (see Unit 1)

Ask the pupils to identify the most significant moment in each scene and discuss how best to express that moment as a freeze-frame. Discuss this moment in relation to the issues in the rest of the play and the kind of atmosphere required. Also consider appropriate characterisation for each character and the relationships between them at this moment in the play. Discuss where each character might be placed on the stage, both in relation to each other and in relation to the audience. Talk about how each character might be feeling at this moment in the play and discuss how characters might communicate these feelings to the audience via verbal and non-verbal expressions. The emphasis should be on communicating with the audience to reflect the atmosphere of the scene and the issues within the whole play.

The character walkabout

Ask each pupil to consider their character's personality and how this might be communicated to an audience through the way the character moves. Then ask pupils to take on the movements of their characters as they walk round the room. Characters should not acknowledge other characters since they need to concentrate on how they move. Repeat this activity with different situations, such as walking as if their character were in a hurry, walking along a beach, feeling angry, bored, happy and so on.

Greetings in role

Ask pupils to consider how their character might speak and how they might relate to acquaintances that they do not know well, for example, will they be friendly or reserved, will they use informal or formal language? Ask pupils to walk around the room in role as their character, but when they meet others they should briefly greet them in a voice and manner appropriate to their character and then move on. This may involve saying *Hello, Hi* or a more formal *How do you do?*, depending on the character. Pupils should use this as an opportunity to develop suitable voices for their characters but should be discouraged from using extreme voices that they will not be able to sustain.

Hot-seating (see Unit 5)

Ask each pupil to assess how their character feels about other characters in the play and how others feel about them. Alternatively use this strategy to develop ideas and thoughts about how the main characters feel about the minor characters and vice versa.

Improvising imaginary situations

Allow pupils to improvise situations showing how their characters might relate to each other in situations other than those in the play. Choose moments of tension such as becoming stuck in a lift, becoming lost or waiting for a train that is delayed.

Thought tracking

Select a short section of the play involving some interaction between characters. Then allocate two pupils per character. Ask one of these two pupils to say a few of their lines and then stop to allow the other pupil to comment on what that character might be thinking at that moment in the play. Alternatively, ask pupils to perform this to the class and ask the class to speculate on the thoughts of each character at various points in the action. This helps pupils become aware of the sub-text.

The silent movie (see Unit 4, Year 9: Shakespeare – The Silent Movie)

If pupils are to perform a longer play, write a brief summary of the main events. Read the summary out loud and ask pupils to respond by quickly walking through the events and miming the actions. The effect is similar to a silent movie, but without the need to move unnaturally fast. Concentrate on making sure the right characters move at the right times, rather than insisting on accuracy of mime or other details. Repeat the activity again so that pupils gain a sense of the whole play and become familiar with the sequence of events. Follow this by asking pupils to identify parts which have potential for tension.

Creating atmosphere through set, lighting and costume

Discuss how the director might create a particular atmosphere through a choice of set, lighting and costume. Ask pupils to suggest set, lighting and costume for particular genres such as horror, romance or pantomime. Ask pupils to suggest set, lighting and costume for contrasting scenes in plays they are studying, for example, in Shakespeare's *Twelfth Night* contrast the atmosphere required for the scene where Malvolio is imprisoned to that required of the scene where Malvolio enters the garden in yellow stockings.

Evaluation – Making Links

Links to the National Curriculum Key Stages 3 and 4 English Programmes of Study

Drama: **S&L 4**   To participate in a range of drama activities and to evaluate their own work and others' contributions, pupils should be taught to . . .
d) evaluate critically performances of dramas they have watched or in which they have taken part.

Breadth of Study
Drama activities 11
The range should include:
c) discussing and reviewing their own and others' performances

 ### Links to the English Framework Objectives

Year 7
Drama: **S&L 19**

Year 8
Drama: **S&L 13, 16**

Year 9
Drama: **S&L 11, 15**

Rationale

The following strategies may be used successfully with all Key Stage 3 year groups to support and develop pupils' knowledge and understanding of how to evaluate their own and other people's dramatic presentations and performances.

Overview

Strategies to Support Evaluation of Performance

Organise short group presentations for evaluation

Build up pupils' knowledge and understanding of how to evaluate a performance by organising short group presentations (see Units 6 and 7 for examples) and then move through the following stages:

a) Model the evaluation process by selecting and explaining one or two points of good practice and one area for development after every performance.

b) Open up discussion by inviting the performers and the audience to select one aspect of the performance they thought worked well.

c) Allow the performers a few minutes to select one aspect of the performance that they thought worked well and one aspect they would like to improve. Invite the performers to share their opinions with the audience.

d) Ask the performers and the audience to select one aspect they thought worked well and one aspect they would like to improve. Then invite the performers and audience to share their views.

e) Ask pupils to make a written evaluation of their group's performance by recording between one and three positive comments and between one and three areas for development.

f) Ask pupils to make a written evaluation similar to point e) but with reference to their own personal performance.

Use freeze-frames, thought tracking and forum theatre (see Unit 1)

These combined strategies help pupils identify the contributions of a director by providing them with directing experience on a small scale. Ask pupils to make decisions on the arrangement of actors, appropriate sets, costumes, props and special effects for freeze-frames, as if they were the directors.

Attend professional performances

Arrange for pupils to see performances by professional companies. Use these experiences to help pupils identify the contributions of the writer, actors and director and identify positive points and areas for development. Use the *Evaluation Guide* on photocopiable sheet 8.2 to support pupils' written evaluations.

UNIT NINE   MANTLE OF THE EXPERT

Making Links

Links to the National Curriculum Key Stages 3 and 4 English Programmes of Study

Drama: **S&L 4**   To participate in a range of drama activities and to evaluate their own and others' contributions, pupils should be taught to use a variety of dramatic techniques to explore ideas, issues, texts and meanings.

Links to the English Framework Objectives

Year 7
Drama: **S&L 16**
Spelling strategies: **Wd 11**

Year 8
Drama: **S&L 15**
Stylistic conventions of non-fiction: **Sn 9**

Year 9
Drama: **S&L 12**
Persuade, argue, advise: **TLW 15**

Definition and Rationale

Pupils are placed in a role with given expertise in a particular subject or area of knowledge, for example, scientists, journalists, eye witnesses to events in a narrative text or colleagues of a character from a story. Pupils are required to provide information to someone who knows less than they do. Being in this role allows the pupils to speak or make decisions with authority, as if expertise has been thrown upon their shoulders like a mantle. By reversing the situation in a typical lesson (where the teacher usually holds the expertise), this strategy has potential to raise pupils' self-esteem, leading to increased levels of motivation and learning.

Year 7   Dangerous Words

A Literacy/Drama Lesson

Main focus: Using multi-sensory re-inforcement to spell words which pose a particular challenge

 Links to the English Framework Objectives for Year 7

Drama:

S&L 16   work collaboratively to devise and present scripted and unscripted pieces, which maintain the attention of the audience

Spelling strategies:

Wd 11   identify words which pose a particular challenge and learn them by using mnemonics, multi-sensory re-inforcement and memorising critical features.

Preparation

1   Organise the class into small groups.
2   Define a small performance area for groups to perform one at a time.
3   Obtain a box and write the title *Dangerous Words* on the outside.
4   Collect about 10 words which pose a particular challenge to the class in terms of spelling and write each word in large letters on a small card.
5   Place the cards in the *Dangerous Words* box.
6   Pupils will need rough paper and writing materials.

Introduction

1   Share the objectives with the class.
2   Show the class the box and explain that it contains words that are 'dangerous' because they are difficult to spell. Ask the class to guess what words might be in the box but do not reveal any just yet.
3   Ask the class to imagine the following scenario: they work for a company that creates chants and jingles for local radio and simple adverts for TV companies. In this role they are experts at making catchy and amusing slogans to sell products. They have been approached by a schools' network to create a video of some chants or jingles based on words that are difficult to spell. The work needs to involve some kind of chant or jingle accompanied by a simple scene or freeze-frame that illustrates the word. It must appeal to pupils between the ages of 10 and 13 and should last no longer than 30 seconds.
4   Organise pupils into their groups and ask a representative from each group to pick out a word from the box. Ask the class to identify why each word is difficult to spell, for example, *vegetable* is difficult to spell because the middle e is an unstressed vowel. Point out that this fact needs to be the focus of jingle or chant.
5   Offer the following as examples:

The Vegetable Chant

VEG   e   table

VEG   e   table

Soon you will be able

To spell your veg e table

With 3 E s

The Lemonade Chant

Do you know

There's an O

In lemonade?

Do you know

There's an O

In lemonade?

There is no I in lemon

There is no U in lemon

Do you know

There's an O

In lemonade?

There's an O

In lemonade!

Suggest a simple scene to illustrate the word and accompany the chant, such as people ordering and drinking lemonade or cooking vegetables.

Development

Set groups the task of devising a simple chant or jingle with a short accompanying scene, based on the word they have chosen from the *Dangerous Words* box. Explain that they will also be asked to perform the chant or jingle to the rest of the class.

Differentiation

1   Support less confident groups by providing them with the chants or jingles beforehand, thus enabling them to concentrate on learning the chant and devising and performing the scene. Use the above chants on *lemonade* or *vegetable* if appropriate. Alternatively, use a published CD resource such as *Dangerous Words* by Larraine and Kerry Harrison (TTS).
2   Challenge more confident groups by asking them to set their jingle to a well known song and/or choose two words to incorporate into one scene.
3   When most groups have something to share with the others, stop the activity and ask them to hold a final rehearsal of the work they have done so far. The chant or jingle or the scene in outline will suffice.

Plenary

1   Ask groups to share or perform their work so far and ask the class to comment on how effective the chants are in helping pupils remember the spellings.
2   Remind pupils of the lesson objectives and focus on the power of multi-sensory material to help people remember how to spell words.

Links to future work

1   Hold a spelling test on the *Dangerous Words* in the chants to see how effective they have been. When most pupils can spell a particular 'dangerous' word, take it out of the *Dangerous Words* box and put it on the wall or in another box entitled *Tamed Words*.
2   Suggest that pupils write down and/or record their chants or jingles on tape and present them as a class book of *Dangerous Words*.
3   Invite some groups to share their chants as a starter activity on spelling next lesson.
4   Suggest that pupils devise chants and jingles to help them spell words that they personally find difficult. Some may like to fit the chants to a pop song.

Year 8   Mrs Canning's Challenge

A Literacy Lesson

Main focus: Exploring the language of advertising as a form of persuasive writing

 Links to the English Framework Objectives for Year 8

Drama:

S&L 15 explore and develop ideas, issues and relationships through work in role

Stylistic conventions of non-fiction:

Sn 9 adapt the stylisitic conventions of the main non-fiction text types to fit different audiences and purposes, e.g. advertisements, documentaries, editorials.

Preparation

1 Organise the class into pairs or threes.
2 Collect a number of small household items in average-to-poor condition that could be offered for sale in a local paper and place them in a shopping bag.
3 Make sufficient copies of the task sheet on photocopiable sheet 9.1; enough for one copy per group.
4 Make sufficient copies of the list of items on photocopiable sheet 9.2; enough for one copy per group.
5 Obtain photocopies of small adverts from the local paper, sufficient for one per pair.
6 You will also need the use of a flipchart or white board.

Introduction

1 Share the lesson objectives with the class.
2 Ask the class to imagine that they work for a charity known as IAS, which stands for Independent Age Support. Explain that the charity is dedicated to helping elderly people help themselves, rather than giving them money or material things.
3 Ask the class to accept that, when you pick up the shopping bag and say the word *ACTION,* you will take on the role of the IAS Co-ordinator, who is in charge of the workers. This will also be a signal for them to take on the role of workers at a meeting. Make it clear that the role play will stop whenever you say the word *FREEZE.*
4 Take on the roles as above and welcome the workers to the meeting. Use the context of photocopiable sheet 9.1 to convey the task of helping an elderly person to advertise some of her possessions. Hand out copies of the list on photocopiable sheet 9.2 and use this to explain the task. Tell the workers that you have been sent some of the items and given a list of others. Ask the workers to advertise the real items first and then go to the list.
5 Take one of the objects from the bag and ask the workers if they have any suggestions on how this could be advertised to make it appear an attractive offer without being totally dishonest. Refer to the examples on the task sheet and hand out the examples from the local paper. Allow pairs a few minutes to read these before asking for suggestions on how to compose a suitable advert for the object. Then devise one on the flipchart or board.

Development

1 Allocate one real object and one listed object to each group to begin to draft the adverts. It is more effective if you can maintain the role play throughout the task, but if you feel you need to revert to teacher, then temporarily stop the role play using the word *FREEZE* and re-start after the pupils have drafted the adverts.
2 As co-ordinator you can move around the groups to support and encourage pupils.

Differentiation

1 Pupils requiring extra support should be given items that are in reasonable condition and less challenging to describe. Give guidance to these pupils concerning what to include in each advert,

for example, description, condition and some persuasive comment such as *bought for £20, a bargain at £15*. Alternatively, pupils requiring support can work with you in a group to produce one advert between them.

2   Pupils requiring more challenge to their powers of persuasion should be given objects in very poor condition that are unlikely to sell well, such as a tin of old spectacles or a stained tea cosy.

Plenary

1   Re-instate the role play if necessary, and invite groups to come together to assess the success of the work so far. Ask groups to select one of their adverts that they feel has the best chance of a sale and invite them to read their advert to the other workers. Discuss reasons why each advert might succeed and suggest any alterations with the class. Thank the workers for their efforts and then stop the activity.

2   Remind the pupils of the lesson objectives and link to the content of this lesson.

Year 9   Living with Mental Illness

A Literacy Lesson

Main Focus: Discussing and writing about a specific social issue

This example focuses on the problems of a young person living with someone who suffers from a mental illness and is designed as a preview to studying a specific text on a similar issue. However the strategy can be applied to a range of other social issues.

 Links to specific texts   *About Face* – a play by Paul Whitfield; *Harry Pushed Her* – a poem by Peter Thabit Jones

Links to the English Framework Objectives for Year 9

Drama:
S&L 12   use a range of drama techniques, including work in role, to explore issues, ideas and meanings . . .

Persuade, argue, advise:
TLW 15   offer general advice or guidelines for action adopting an impersonal style to suggest impartiality and authority.

Preparation

1   You will need the use of a flipchart or board and pupils will need writing materials.
2   Make sufficient copies of photocopiable sheet 9.3 for pairs of pupils.
3   Organise the class into pairs who can support each other with a writing task.
4   Make copies of the poem on photocopiable sheet 6.4 (see Unit 6, Year 8: Spotlighting) or obtain copies of *About Face* by Paul Whitfield (optional).

Introduction

1   Share the lesson objectives with the class,
2   Ask the class to imagine that they are journalists who work on a magazine for young people called *Kudos*. Explain that every month the magazine selects a letter from the problem page that focuses on an issue of general interest to their readers. They then produce a half-page feature which includes some guidance on dealing with the issue. They have recently dealt with issues of bullying and dieting but now intend to focus on the issue of living with a family member who is mentally ill. Explain that the journalists' task will be to discuss the feature and decide on the guidance they will give.
3   Ask the class to accept that when you say the word *ACTION*, you will play the part of the chief editor of *Kudos* and they should take on the roles of the journalists at a meeting about the feature article on living with mental illness. Make it clear that the role play will continue until you say the word *FREEZE*.

Development

1 Take on the role of the chief editor and welcome the journalists to the meeting to discuss the new feature article on living with mental illness. Hand out copies of the problem page letter (on photocopiable sheet 9.3) and read it aloud to the journalists. Discuss some of the issues raised in the letter that could be included in the feature article. Make it clear that whilst the letter will be published in the article, the article will offer general advice to people who have similar problems.

2 Allow the journalists a few minutes to suggest between one and three pieces of advice for people in Jo's situation.

3 Take feedback from pairs and make a list of advice in note form on the flipchart for future reference.

4 Discuss the need to offer impartial advice with confidence, when writing the advice in the feature.

5 Discuss the way the feature might be organised to attract the average reader and take suggestions on how the letter might be incorporated into the text.

The writing task

Stop the role play using the word *FREEZE* as agreed and set one of the following writing tasks:

Either ask the pupils to work in pairs to produce a draft version of the section of the feature that gives advice. Ask pupils to use the list of agreed points (already on the flipchart) as a guide and encourage them to refer to the letter.

Or ask pupils to draft a reply to Jo for the problem page, which incorporates the list of advice.

Plenary

1 Link the problem page letter with issues in other texts such as the situation in the poem *Harry Pushed Her* by Peter Thabit Jones (on photocopiable sheet 6.4) or the issues explored in the play *About Face* by Paul Whitfield. Hand out copies of the poem and read it aloud to the class or read an extract from the play. Ask for pupils' comments on how this text relates to the content of this lesson.

2 Remind the pupils of the lesson objectives and link to the work so far.

Links to future work

1 Ask pupils to complete their draft pieces of advice for homework or during the next lesson.

2 Return to a more detailed study of the poem or play in the light of the discussions in this lesson.

UNIT TEN   WHOLE GROUP DRAMA – PUTTING IT ALL TOGETHER

Making Links

Links to the National Curriculum Key Stages 3 & 4 English Programmes of Study

Knowledge Skills and Understanding

Drama: **S&L 4**   To participate in a range of drama activities and to evaluate their own and others' contributions, pupils should be taught to:

a) use a variety of dramatic techniques to explore ideas, issues, texts and meanings

b) use different ways to convey action, character, atmosphere and tension when they are scripting and performing plays

c) appreciate how the structure and organisation of scenes and plays contribute to dramatic effect

d) evaluate critically performances that they have watched or in which they have taken part.

Breadth of Study

Drama activities 11

The range should include:

a) improvisation and working in role

b) devising, scripting and performing plays

c) discussing and reviewing their own and others' performances.

 ### Links to the English Framework Objectives

Year 7
Drama: **S&L 15, 16, 17, 18, 19**
Study of literary texts: **TLR 19**
Plan, draft and present: **TLW 1**
Inform, explain, describe: **TLW 14**

Year 8
Drama: **S&L 13, 14, 15, 16**
Study of literary texts: **TLR 16**
Plan, draft and present: **TLW 2**
Inform, explain, describe: **TLW 12**

Year 9
Drama: **S&L 11, 12, 14**
Plan, draft and present: **TLW 2**

Definition, Rationale and Elaboration

1   Whole group drama is where all the pupils, and sometimes the teacher, behave and respond as if they were living inside an imaginary situation. Those within the whole group drama are expected to respond appropriately according to the dramatic context. This approach enables the teacher to structure the drama to build up belief and create depths of thought and feeling.

2   Whole group drama has considerable flexibility in that it can be stopped and re-started, thus allowing pupils to reflect upon the work as it proceeds. It has the capacity to allow pupils to dwell on a significant moment in the present or explore events in the past or the future.

3   The overarching nature of this strategy means that it has the capacity to incorporate many of the drama strategies referred to in this book, such as freeze-frames, hot-seating and the writing and performing of

scripted drama. This affords an ideal context within which pupils can develop their understanding of a range of drama techniques and evaluate their own levels of participation, both verbally and in writing.

4   Through whole group drama, the teacher can create life-like situations which encourage motivation and commitment, stimulate language and broaden pupils' understanding by working from the inside of imaginary contexts. Inside whole group drama, pupils can take a wide variety of roles, including adult roles of responsibility that often demand different language registers and the skills of co-operation, negotiation and problem solving.

5   Situations for whole group drama can arise from English texts or other curriculum subjects such as history and geography.

Making the Whole Group Drama Contract

Why pupils need a contract

Whole group drama can be a powerful teaching strategy, especially when linked to teacher-in-role. However, it requires careful planning and an initial agreement or contract for all concerned to enter into the dramatic framework with integrity and sensitivity. The contract is important to ensure that the work is treated with sufficient respect to allow depths of feeling and analysis to develop.

Introducing the contract

Making a contract at the beginning of the lesson constitutes a verbal agreement for the teacher and the pupils to enter into the imaginary world of the drama with integrity. Most pupils enjoy drama and can appreciate the need for such an agreement, providing it is presented in a positive manner. The tone of the teacher's voice and the manner of delivery when introducing the contract is the key to its success. A firm, clear but positive explanation of the contract works best, along with a tone of voice that assumes co-operation. In most cases the contract merely involves asking the pupils to agree to play the roles of different people in a different place and time, in order to conduct the drama work. If pupils need further explanation about whole group drama, it can be compared to taking part in a television reconstruction or making an imaginary video or TV programme. It may also be useful to point out that learning through taking part in dramatic situations is an acknowledged method of training in organisations such as the army, the police force and corporate businesses. Such comparisons with the media and the adult world help to make the prospect of entering the drama more acceptable, if pupils seem cautious.

Dealing with refusals

If a pupil refuses to accept the contract, inform them that the alternative is to sit at the side of the room to observe the drama and take notes to record the events, which will be checked later. It is advisable not to make a fuss about the non-complier. The teacher needs to make it an easier and more attractive prospect to agree to the contract than to opt out.

Dealing with pupils who break the contract

Incorporate clear signals into the contract, for stopping and starting the drama so that it is relatively easy to stop the drama should a pupil start to behave inappropriately. The *ACTION/FREEZE* commands are the most common signals.

If a pupil breaks the contract by behaving inappropriately, either have a quiet word with them during the drama when others are occupied, stop the drama and speak to the pupil directly, or target the behaviour via a reminder for the whole class. Sometimes it is possible to regulate inappropriate behaviour within the drama, if the teacher is in role. However, if the inappropriate behaviour persists after a warning, then the offending pupil should be asked to sit at the side of the room and asked to complete a written task for a set time. After this time, you may want to offer the pupil the opportunity to re-make the contract and return to the drama. Whole group drama can take place in one lesson, but works best where it becomes a holding form for a series of lessons on the same theme. A whole group drama theme can last up to half a term, with drama and literacy lessons running alongside each other. It creates an ongoing audience and purpose for pieces of written work, which pupils often take on board with enthusiasm, due to high levels of engagement in the dramatic context.

Years 7, 8 & 9   *CHARLOTTE DYMOND*

A series of Literacy/Drama Lessons

Link with specific text and main textual focus: *The Ballad of Charlotte Dymond* by Charles Causley

This strategy acts as a potential holding form for all the other strategies in this book.

The following example constitutes a series of literacy/drama lessons that can be applied to, or adapted to suit, any narrative text in Years 7, 8 and 9.

Links to the English Framework Objectives for Year 7

Drama:

S&L 15   develop drama techniques to explore in role a variety of situations and texts or respond to stimuli

S&L 16   work collaboratively to devise and present scripted and unscripted pieces, which maintain the attention of an audience

S&L 17   extend their spoken repertoire by experimenting with language in different roles and dramatic contexts

S&L 18   develop drama techniques and strategies for anticipating, visualising and problem-solving in different learning contexts

S&L 19   reflect on and evaluate their own presentations and those of others

Study of literary texts:

TLR 19   explore how form contributes to meaning in poems from different times and cultures, e.g. *storytelling in ballads*

Plan, draft and present:

TLW 1   plan, draft, edit, revise, proofread and present a text with readers and purpose in mind

Inform, explain, describe:

TLW 14   describe an object, person or setting in a way that includes relevant details and is accurate and evocative.

Links to the English Framework Objectives for Year 8

Drama:

S&L 13   reflect on their participation in drama and identify areas for their development of dramatic techniques, e.g. *keep a reflective record of their contributions to dramatic improvisation and presentation*

S&L 14   develop the dramatic techniques that enable them to create and sustain a variety of roles

S&L 15   explore and develop ideas, issues and relationships through work in role

S&L 16   collaborate in, and evaluate, the presentation of dramatic performances, scripted and unscripted, which explore character, relationships and issues

Study of literary texts:

TLR 16   recognise how texts refer to and reflect the culture in which they were produced, e.g. *in their evocation of place and values*

Plan, draft and present:

TLW 2   re-read work to anticipate the effect on the reader and revise style and structure, as well as accuracy with this in mind

Inform, explain, describe:

TLW 12   describe an event, process or situation, using language with an appropriate degree of formality.

....

Links to the English Framework Objectives for Year 9

Drama:

S&L 11 recognise, evaluate and extend the skills and techniques they have developed through drama

S&L 12 use a range of drama techniques, including work in role, to explore issues, ideas and meanings...

S&L 14 convey action, character, atmosphere and tension when scripting and performing plays

Plan, draft and present:

TLW 2 record, develop and evaluate ideas through writing.

....

Preparation for the following Lessons 1–8

1 Make sufficient copies of the poem on photocopiable sheet 10.1 for every pupil, but do not allow pupils to read the poem until indicated in these lesson notes i.e. towards the end of the lessons. The aim is twofold:

   a) to familiarise the pupils with the issues and events in the poem *before* they read it in ballad form

   b) to enable them to record the events in the form of news articles allowing a comparison between modern news telling and ballad form.

2 You will need an item of clothing to represent a young man from 100 years ago, such as a cloth cap, waistcoat or cravat. You will also need a plain scarf and a patterned cloth the size of a shawl that looks like it could have been worn 100 years ago.

3 Obtain as many of the following props as you can: a small string of old fashioned pearls or beads, four silver coins, a cloth purse made of old fashioned material, a piece of bright yellow material (any size). Place these props in a bag and take to **Lesson 1**, but keep them out of sight until needed.

4 Designate a small performance space large enough for one small group to stand in a line or a cluster.

5 Draw a large thought bubble on an A4 sheet and place this in a plastic pocket.

6 Draw a large heart on an A4 sheet and place this in a plastic pocket.

7 Pupils will need writing materials at various points in the sequence of lessons.

Lesson 1

Introduction

1 Explain that this is the first in a series of lessons that centre on the events and theme of a narrative poem. Make it clear that the poem is written in slightly old-fashioned language and will remain a secret until the last lessons, so the pupils will be familiar with the events before they attempt to understand the language.

2 Share the objectives for the series of lessons with the class.

(Year 8 and 9 only) drama diaries or log books

Explain that the class will be using a series of drama techniques to explore this poem over the next few lessons. Set up the concept of a drama diary or logbook so that they can identify, evaluate and select areas where they need to develop their drama skills alongside the study of the poem.

Making the whole group drama contract

Ask the pupils to take on the roles of investigative journalists in relation to a murder that happened in 1870. Then explain the following to the class:

The story in the unspecified poem centres around a crime, based on a real-life event that happened around 1870. The crime involves the murder of a young woman by the name of Charlotte Dymond. Ask the class if they will agree to take on the roles of journalists investigating a reconstruction of events leading up to the crime. The purpose of the re-investigation is to assess whether the person convicted of the crime in the 1870s was guilty or not. Explain that because we have no records of the police investigations, some of the reconstruction will be based on evidence from the poem and some will be based on what we feel could have happened.

Use signal words such as *ACTION* and *FREEZE* to indicate when the pupils should be in and out of role. Place the bag of props where you can reach it and then start the role play. Adopt a formal court style language to set the tone, as you present the investigators with 'some of the evidence available to the police on the day after the crime'.

Your explanation may begin as follows:

The body of a young woman was discovered in some marshes near the Cornish town of Bodmin on a Monday in April. The exact date is unknown but thought to be around the year 1870. The body was found clothed in the following items. Obviously, we do not have the exact items but we have similar items to give you an idea of what they were like. (Bring out the relevant items from the bag as you refer to them.)

Exhibit A – a diamond shawl

Exhibit B – a yellow gown or dress

Exhibit C – a necklace of beads

Exhibit D – four silver shillings in a purse

Explain that the woman was found with her throat cut in a thin line around her beads, which were covered in blood. Point out that as her money was not taken, the motive was not likely to be robbery.

Development

1 Tell the journalists that according to the evidence, the murdered woman was last seen on a Sunday night by someone who lived in her house. Explain that the identity of this person is not known, but for the purposes of this re-investigation the journalists are asked to accept that it was Charlotte's sister (change this to her brother if you are a male teacher).

2 Inform the journalists that they will be given the opportunity to interview yourself in role as Charlotte's sister/brother the day after the body was found. Explain that this is part of the re-investigation. Ask the pupils if they are willing to accept you in role as this person. Most pupils will readily accept this, but should anyone refuse, ask them to sit at the side and observe instead of taking part.

Hot-seating a teacher-in-role (see Unit 5)

1 Bring out the scarf. Explain that you will play the part of this person for as long as you wear the scarf. Ask the journalists what they feel Charlotte's sister might know, that could be useful to them in writing their first article about the re-investigation of this case. Discuss some ideas and then ask the journalists to spend a few minutes in pairs preparing three to four suitable questions that they would like Charlotte's sister to answer. These should be written down in note form as they are discussed.

2 Ask for a volunteer to ask the first question. Ask the journalists to tick off the questions on their sheet if someone else asks them. Emphasise that they should be interested in the answers rather than who asks the questions. After the first question, anyone else can ask a question but they should not call out over each other, or they may miss something important. Suggest that they raise their hands if they have a question. Warn the journalists not to assume that the sister will always be honest with them and tell them everything she knows. It will be up to them to ask her more questions if they are not satisfied with her answers.

3 Sit in a chair at the front of the class and take on the role of Charlotte's sister. Play the role with integrity in order to build belief in the dramatic context.

Answer the questions and/or volunteer information to make sure you *gradually* reveal the following key information based on the events in the poem. Reveal enough to keep the pupils interested but don't give too much away too soon.

Information about Charlotte's relationship with Matthew

Charlotte always went walking with her boyfriend Matthew after tea on Sundays. Matthew walked with a limp. Hint that you were surprised that Charlotte was attracted to him. Admit that Charlotte was popular with other boys and they may have asked her out whilst she was seeing Matthew. Be evasive about this and if put under pressure emphasise that you don't know if she was unfaithful or not. Hint or suggest that Matthew could be sensitive and was a loner because of his disability. Inform them that he appeared to be very possessive with Charlotte.

If asked, you are unsure how Matthew acquired a limp.

Information about Matthew the day after the murder
Tell the journalists that you went to see Matthew the day after the murder, but he refused to speak. His face was pale and he was sewing a tear in his clothes but he would not talk to anyone. He just kept crying and wiping his face with a green handkerchief. Tell the journalists that the handkerchief was very like the one Charlotte had recently bought in Bodmin town.

Information about the night of the murder
Tell them that you remember that even though it was raining that Sunday night, Charlotte went out to the marshes with Matthew. He was leaning on her arm because of his limp. Emphasise how smart she looked in her best Sunday clothes – her yellow gown, and her favourite shawl and beads. Describe how Charlotte was found with her Sunday beads covered in blood and how the police constable told the family that the deadly cut looked like it had been made with a razor.

4   When you have revealed all the information above, tell the journalists that you have to leave and then stop the interview by taking off the scarf and saying *FREEZE*.

Reflection to consolidate the learning and support belief and commitment for the next activity
Allow the journalists a few minutes to work in pairs to discuss what they have discovered or suspect as a result of the interview with Charlotte's sister. Then take feedback to open up discussion and ask the group to select the most interesting information for their first newspaper article on the re-investigation of the crime.

Freeze-frame, and forum theatre (see Unit 1)
1   Refer to the need to consider audience and purpose and then suggest that, in the absence of any photographs, they use an artist's impression of Charlotte, with the caption *Charlotte Dymond with her family in happier times* underneath.
2   Stop the role play using the word *FREEZE* and suggest that a group of pupils make a freeze-frame at the front of the class to indicate what the artist's impression might look like. Write the caption on the board and ask the class to suggest what could constitute a *happy time* for Charlotte and her family. Suggest events such as a birthday or a family outing if pupils find this difficult to decide. Ask pupils to decide whether Matthew might be in the picture. Ask some pupils to volunteer to represent the characters in the freeze-frame and ask the class to make the key decisions about where each character should be looking and why. Discuss how the characters might be feeling and decide on the expressions on their faces. Finally, ask the pupils to make the freeze-frame and hold it to the count of 5 to consider the effect of the image as an artist's impression in a newspaper.

Introducing the writing task
1   Explain that during the next lesson, pupils will be expected to complete a short draft of a newspaper article about the re-investigation of the case. The article should include the facts of the case and what they discovered from the interview with Charlotte's sister. They should include a headline and an artist's impression roughly based on the freeze-frame and caption on the board.
2   Take some suggestions for headlines if necessary and ask the class to prepare for the next lesson by working in pairs to help each other create their headlines. Pairs may use the same headlines if they wish. Allow a few minutes for this with an extension task of starting to sketch the artist's impression.

Plenary

1 (**Year 7 only**) Ask each pair to share their headlines with the rest of the class.
2 Allow pairs a few minutes to record between three and five major facts about the murder that need to be included in their newspaper articles, and between one and three opinions or suspicions. Take brief feedback.
3 Identify the drama techniques used in this lesson as hot-seating and freeze-frames with forum theatre.
4 (**Years 8 and 9 only**) Ask pupils to record these drama techniques in their drama diaries or log books. Discuss the skills involved in devising and asking appropriate questions in the hot-seating, and performing or analysing character's positions and feelings in the freeze-frame. Allow pupils a few minutes to evaluate how they personally contributed to these techniques, in preparation for the homework task of filling in the diary.

Homework suggestions

1 **Years 7:** Pupils should complete a suitable artist's impression for their article, along with the caption and the final headline.
2 **Years 8 and 9:** Pupils should complete their drama diaries or log books, to define the techniques and evaluate their individual contributions.

Overview of Follow up Lessons

Lesson 2

Pupils edit and complete final versions of their articles on the circumstances surrounding the Charlotte Dymond murder.

Introduction

1 Allow the class 1 to 2 minutes to work in pairs to recall and note down between three and five facts about the murder that would need to be included in their article. Then take feedback and make a list of facts on the board.
2 **Model Writing:** Take one of the facts and model how to write it in the style of a newspaper article.
3 **Shared Writing:** Ask the class to help you compose a second fact in a similar style, linked to the first.
4 **Application:** Select a third fact and give the class 1 minute to work as individuals to draft this into a suitable sentence that links to the other two. Use whiteboards if available. Take feedback to assess their levels of understanding and select examples of good practice.
5 Work with the class to suggest an order for the facts to appear in an article and number them accordingly. Emphasise that this order is only a suggestion.

Development

Ask pupils to work as individuals to draft, edit and complete a final version of their article.

Differentiation

1 Support less confident pupils by suggesting that they keep to the order of facts on the board and write one clear sentence about each fact.
2 Challenge more confident pupils to make the facts more interesting and/or intriguing by changing the order in which the facts are presented and using appropriate adverbs and adjectives.

Plenary

Ask pupils to select the best part of their article. Then, ask a few pupils to read out some of their work and use this to emphasise features of newspaper style writing.

Lessons 3 and 4

The task for the next two lessons is to explore the character of Matthew in order to write an article about him in the light of the following latest news: Matthew is now under suspicion for the murder of Charlotte Dymond, but has gone missing.

Hot-seating (see Unit 5)

1   Use hot-seating to enable the journalists to question Matthew and Charlotte's friends. The objective is to discover more about Matthew's personality and his relationship with Charlotte during the weeks before the murder and also to discover the perspectives of friends and acquaintances of Charlotte and Matthew. Up to half the class can play the parts of the friends.

2   Allow a few minutes for each group to prepare. They should work in pairs for this task. Ask the journalists to devise questions for the friends. Ask the friends to decide on how well they know each of the characters and then invent information and observations about the couple.

3   Chair the hot-seating but intervene occasionally if necessary to enable points to be made clearly or to ask a probing question.

4   Stop the hot-seating and ask the class to summarise what the hot-seating has revealed about Matthew that could be useful for the article. Note the main points on the board.

The writing task

Agree on a headline that informs the readers that Matthew is under suspicion and is missing. Discuss a suitable picture to accompany the article, such as an artist's' impression of Matthew walking with Charlotte and agree on a caption. Ask pupils to work as individuals to write their articles under this headline. After writing the article, ask them to make a rough sketch of the picture for an artist to use as a guide.

Lessons 5 and 6

The task for the next two lessons is to write a short play script, which reflects the views of the neighbours about the couple, one week before the murder.

Use this task as an opportunity to discuss how people's attitudes to disability have changed since the 1870s. Make it clear that the neighbours may hold opinions about Matthew's disability that would not be considered appropriate today. If you have pupils in the class who are physically disabled, discuss this with them before the lesson to minimise any unintentional offence. Alternatively, ask the class to avoid any offensive references to Matthew's disability.

Spotlighting (see Unit 6)

1   Set the scene as the Sunday before the murder, when Charlotte and Matthew set off towards the marshes on their usual walk. Ask pupils to speculate on what the neighbours might have said about the couple as they passed by each of their windows en route to the marshes. Keep this brief and then allow groups to improvise a conversation as if the couple were passing their window. Ask them to play the parts of adults who are from the same family, or friends. The improvisation should last no more than 30 seconds and everyone in the group should have a speaking part. Encourage pupils to consider how to convey action, character, atmosphere and tension in their work (see points in Unit 6 on the spotlighting process).

2   Allow pupils time to hold a final rehearsal. Then invite two pupils to represent the couple and ask them to walk around the room, stopping at each group to bring their conversation to life. Select two different pupils to play the couple when these pupils reach their own group, so they can participate in their improvisation.

The writing task

1   Ask pupils to write a play script based roughly on their improvisations. Split the groups up to allow pupils to work in pairs. Ask them to produce one script per pair, taking turns to scribe. They may adapt their original improvisation if they wish to do so.

2   Remind pupils to convey character, tension and so on in their play scripts.

Plenary

Year 7
Ask a few pupils to read out their draft scripts and use these to discuss good practice.

Years 8 and 9
1 Discuss and list the skills necessary for effective improvisation as a drama technique. Ask pupils to record these in their drama diaries or log books and allow them a few minutes to evaluate and make notes on their own contributions to the improvisations during this lesson.
2 Repeat the process above, focusing on the writing of play scripts.

Homework suggestion (for Years 8 and 9 only)
Pupils fill in drama log books based on the above techniques.

Lessons 7 and 8
The pupils are invited to form an opinion about Matthew's guilt and are introduced to the poem to discover the verdict. They are invited to compare how the facts were presented at the time, in the form of a ballad, as opposed to their own newspaper articles. Use these lessons to focus on the study of the ballad form as a means of spreading news in the past.

1 Ask the class to summarise the neighbours' opinions about the couple and discuss any theories about Matthew's motives for the murder.
2 Inform the class of the next piece of news that Matthew was caught by police trying to escape on a ship off the coast of Plymouth and is now in police custody. He is about to go on trial for the murder of Charlotte Dymond.
3 Allow pupils a few minutes in pairs to discuss their response to this news and consider whether they think Matthew should be found guilty of murder or manslaughter if they feel he was to blame.
4 Introduce the poem (see photocopiable sheet 10.1) and ask the class to follow as you read it, to discover the verdict and the sentence. Discuss the verdict and what might have occurred today.
5 Then read the poem to the class again, as pupils follow the words. As they listen and follow the poem, ask pupils to consider the key differences between how the story is revealed in ballad form compared to their news articles. List the key differences and then list the features of the ballad form alongside the features of the newspaper style. Then consider the advantages and disadvantages of spreading news in ballad form and discuss the context of the ballad form.
6 Follow this with an appreciation of the poem in terms of the figurative language and other aspects of the ballad.

Suggestions for future lessons
Years 8 and 9 should complete drama diaries or log books after, or during the plenary of each lesson where they have been involved in particular drama techniques.

Thought tracking (see Unit 1)
1 Ask pupils to script comments made by people at Charlotte's funeral and comments made at Matthew's funeral to link with the last few lines of the poem.
2 These comments can be recorded onto an audio cassette tape. The tape can begin with a few lines from the funeral service to set the scene, followed by the people's comments.

Whole class improvisation
1 Plan and perform a reconstruction of Matthew's trial. Allocate parts for the whole class as witnesses, council for the prosecution and defence, court officials and jury.
2 Involve the whole class in devising appropriate language and some of the questions for the various courtroom roles. Then allow individuals to work out their questions and stories for the court. Each pupil with a courtroom speaking part should be supported by a partner who has a less challenging speaking part.
3 Allow pupils to use simple items of costume to perform the role play and video the proceedings or take photographs if equipment is available.

Writing task
Reflect and write evaluations on the performance after the event. Note, at the end of the series of lessons, return to the lesson objectives and link to the content of the work.

PHOTOCOPIABLE SHEETS

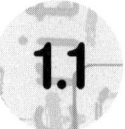

1.1 YEAR 7 EVACUEES WRITE HOME

Extract from *Goodnight Mr Tom* by Michelle Magorian

Meeting

'Yes,' said Tom bluntly, on opening the front door. 'What d'you want?'

A harassed middle-aged woman in a green coat and felt hat stood on his step. He glanced at the armband on her sleeve. She gave him an awkward smile.

'I'm the Billeting Officer for this area,' she began.

'Oh yes, and what's that got to do wi' me?'

She flushed slightly. 'Well, Mr, Mr . . .'

'Oakley. Thomas Oakley.'

'Ah, thank you, Mr Oakley.' She paused and took a deep breath. 'Mr Oakley, with the declaration of war imminent . . .'

Tom waved his hand. 'I knows all that. Git to the point. What d'you want?' He noticed a small boy at her side.

'It's him I've come about,' she said. 'I'm on my way to your village hall with the others.'

'What others?'

She stepped to one side. Behind the large iron gate which stood at the end of the graveyard were a small group of children. Many of them were filthy and very poorly clad. Only a handful had a blazer or coat. They all looked bewildered and exhausted. One tiny dark-haired girl in the front was hanging firmly on to a new teddy-bear.

The woman touched the boy at her side and pushed him forward.

'There's no need to tell me,' said Tom. 'It's obligatory and it's for the war effort.'

'You are entitled to choose your child, I know,' began the woman apologetically.

Tom gave a snort.

'But,' she continued, 'his mother wants him to be with someone who's religious or near a church. She was quite adamant. Said she would only let him be evacuated if he was.'

'Was what?' asked Tom impatiently.

'Near a church.'

Tom took a second look at the child. The boy was thin and sickly-looking, pale with limp sandy hair and dull grey eyes.

'His name's Willie,' said the woman.

Willie, who had been staring at the ground, looked up. Round his neck, hanging from a piece of string, was a cardboard label. It read 'William Beech'.

Tom was well into his sixties, a healthy, robust, stockily-built man with a head of thick white hair. Although he was of average height, in Willie's eyes he was a towering giant with skin like coarse, wrinkled brown paper and a voice like thunder.

He glared at Willie. 'You'd best come in,' he said abruptly.

The woman gave a relieved smile. 'Thank you so much,' she said, and she backed quickly away and hurried down the tiny path towards the other children. <u>Willie watched her go.</u>

'Come on in,' repeated Tom harshly. 'I ent got all day.'

 **1.2 YEAR 7 EVACUEES WRITE HOME**

Response Sheet

Record your responses to the text from *Goodnight Mr Tom* by filling in the sections below.

Fill in what occurs to you as you listen to the text read aloud.

You can use pictures, words or diagrams in any of the sections.

As you listen to the text, record:

1 the pictures or images you see in your mind

2 what you imagine you can hear, smell, taste

3 how it makes you feel

4 what it reminds you of

1.3 YEAR 7 EVACUEES WRITE HOME

This is a photograph of some evacuees.
Imagine that you and your partner are two of these evacuees from the same family. Imagine that you were watching when Willie was taken to Tom's house. Decide how you felt when you saw Willie taken to Tom's house and write about what happened in a short letter home. Read the helpline section below and then write one letter between you but take turns to write.

Helpline Section

Consider these questions when you plan what to include in your letter.

How did you feel when you saw Tom answer the door? Why did you feel like this?
Did you feel sorry for Willie or were you just glad that it was not you?
How do you think Tom will treat Willie?

Use *one* of the following suggestions to begin your letter, or make up your own beginning.

1 Dear All,
We liked the train ride but we were very scared when we got here. We had to go round the houses with a woman in a green hat. William Beech's mum said he had to be with someone who lived near a church, so we went there first. A man called Tom came to the door ...

2 Dear Everyone,
It was a tiring journey but we have arrived at our new house. It's not like home but at least we are together. We're glad we aren't staying with a man called Tom. We all went with the billeting officer who took William Beech to Tom's door ...

1.4a YEAR 8 DETECTING THE BIAS

Extract from *Stone Cold* by Robert Swindells

You can call me Link. It's not my name, but it's what I say when anybody asks, which isn't often. I'm invisible, see? One of the invisible people. Right now I'm sitting in a doorway watching the passers-by. They avoid looking at me. They're afraid I want something they've got, and they're right. Also, they don't want to think about me. They don't like reminding I exist. Me, and those like me. We're living proof that everything's not all right and we make the place untidy.

Hang about and I'll tell you the story of my fascinating life . . . I didn't come to London straightaway. I may be homeless and unemployed but I'm not stupid. I'd read about London. I knew the streets down here weren't paved with gold. I knew there were hundreds of people – thousands, in fact – sleeping rough and begging for coppers. But that's just the point, see? In Bradford I stuck out like a sore thumb because there weren't many of us. The police down here have got used to seeing kids kipping in doorways, and mostly they leave you alone. In Bradford I was getting moved on every hour or so. I was getting no sleep at all, and practically no money. People up there haven't got used to beggars yet. They're embarrassed. They'll make large detours to avoid passing close to you, and if somebody does come within earshot and you ask for change, they look startled and hurry on by.

Also, I kept seeing people I knew. Neighbours. Guys I'd been at school with. I even saw one of my teachers once. And if you've never been caught begging by someone who knew you before, you can't possibly know how low it makes you feel.

I wasn't out every night, back then. That was the one good thing about it. Once or twice a week I'd show up at my sister's for a bath, a meal and a decent night's sleep. Trouble was, I was getting scruffier and scruffier, which happens if you sleep in your clothes, and Chris, Carole's feller, got resentful of my visits. He didn't actually say anything to me, but I could see it in his eyes and hear it in his tone of voice, and I knew Carole must be catching hell from him every time I'd been there. So what with one thing and another, I decided it was time to move on.

Sounds good, right? Time to move on. Reminds you of all those old songs about the restless character who hates to stay too long in one place. He meets a girl who falls in love with him, but after a while he hears the old highway calling and so he slings his bed-roll over his shoulder and moves on, leaving the girl to grieve. Dead romantic, eh?

Forget it. Sad, is what it is. Sad and scary. You're leaving a place you know and heading into the unknown with nothing to protect you. No money. No prospect of work. No address where folks will make you welcome. You're going to find yourself living among hard, violent people, some of whom are deranged. You're going to be at risk every minute, day and night. Especially night. There are guys so desperate or so crazy, they'll knife you or batter your head in for your sleeping bag and the coppers you've got in your pocket. There are some who'll try to get in your sleeping-bag with you, because you're a nice-looking lad with soft skin and no stubble. And there's nowhere you can run to, because nobody cares. Nobody gives a damn. You're just another dosser, and one dosser more or less makes no difference.

1.4b YEAR 8 DETECTING THE BIAS

Extract from *Stone Cold* by Robert Swindells

Daily Routine Orders 3

I've been out tonight. I took the tube down to Charing Cross and walked about a bit. Tour of inspection, you might say. And I found them, as I'd known I would. Hundreds of the scruffy blighters, lying around making the place look manky. I marched along the Strand and there they were, dossing in all the doorways – even Lloyds Bank and the Law Courts. <u>One cheeky little bugger – couldn't have been more than seventeen – actually asked me for money.</u> Have you got any change, he says. I looked him up and down and I said, 'Change? I'd change you, my lad, if I had you in khaki for six weeks.' It didn't go in, though. He just smiled and said have a nice night. Cracker up his arse, that's what he wants. That'd wake him up. That, or six weeks at Strensall.

National Service. That was the thing. It brought 'em all in – the teds, the rockers, the Mammy's boys. And it changed 'em, by golly it did. In six weeks. There were no teddy boys on that passing-out parade I can tell you, and no rockers, either. Soldiers, that's what it made of 'em. There were no exceptions.

And that was my mission in life – to turn dirty, scruffy, pimply youths into soldiers. Into men. And I did it, too. Year after year.

Yes, and what thanks do I get? I'll tell you. They chuck me out. Twenty-nine years' service and they turn round and chuck me out. Medical grounds, it says on the chit. Discharged on medical grounds. And there's nothing wrong with me. Nothing. I'm forty-seven and fit as a butcher's dog.

Medical grounds is just an excuse, of course. I know why they really chucked me out. They chucked me out because their mission in life is exactly the opposite of mine. They think I don't know that, but I do. They're all part of the plot, see? There's a plot – it's been hatching a long time now – to undermine the country by clogging it up with dossers and junkies and drunks. Some of the top politicians are in it, and civil servants and social workers and even the church. They want to flood the country with winos and crims and down-and-outs and drag it down till it's no better than some of the filthy holes I've served in all these years. They're powerful, and they'll stop at nothing. What's the career of one Sergeant-Major to them? Nothing, that's what. Nothing.

They're not going to stop me, though. Oh, no. They abolished National Service, and they've put me where I can't turn garbage into men anymore, but I can clean up the garbage, can't I? They can't stop me doing that, and I will. By golly I will.

1.5 YEAR 8 DETECTING THE BIAS

Identify which headlines and captions were printed in which newspaper.
Read their editorial policies to give you some clues.

THE GOVERNOR

The Governor aims to attract law-abiding readers who care for their country and respect its past and future.
The Governor will report the facts.
The Governor supports the rule of Law and Order to make the country run smoothly.
The Governor respects hardworking people.

THE PEOPLE'S VOICE

The People's Voice aims to attract caring readers.
The People's Voice will report the facts.
The People's Voice will support the poor and needy.
The People's Voice will challenge anyone in authority who abuses their power.

THE CITY INDEPENDENT

The City Independent aims to attract fair-minded readers.
The City Independent will report all the facts.
The City Independent will attempt to provide a balanced view.

Write the initials of the paper in the box next to each example:

Article One

Article Two

JUDGE'S ONLY DAUGHTER SENT TO JAIL

Ungrateful Helen Stevens stole money from her doting father Judge Stevens, to pay off her gambling debts. 'If she'd asked for the money I would have helped her' said poor Judge Stevens . . .

CRUEL JUDGE PUTS DAUGHTER IN JAIL

Heartless Judge Stevens had his only daughter arrested for borrowing money to pay off threatening debt collectors. The cruel father let his loving daughter go to a life of hell in jail for borrowing a few pounds . . .

Article Three

JUDGE'S DAUGHTER SENT TO JAIL

Helen Stevens, only daughter of Judge Stevens was sent to jail today for taking money from her father's credit card to pay off her debts. Her father says he reported the crime in an effort to save his daughter from the criminal world. Helen claims she was just borrowing the money and intends to appeal against her conviction . . .

1.6 YEAR 8 DETECTING THE BIAS

Copies of unfinished articles for the attention of the Chief Editors of the
_____ Newspaper.
Select and complete the best article to accompany the photograph of the homeless asking for money.
Please select and complete only ONE of the following articles.
Please ensure that the article is in line with our editorial policy.

Article One

PITY THE HOMELESS – IT COULD BE YOU

Few people set out to become homeless. So how does it happen that so many people end up begging for a crust and how many of us just walk by and ignore them? The poor victims in this photograph only asked the man for some change but he ...

Article Two

WE LIVE IN TERROR ON OUR STREETS

Homeless people are dossers who should get themselves a job like every other law-abiding citizen. Filthy homeless youths frighten honest people by ...

Article Three

NUMBER OF HOMELESS ON THE INCREASE

The number of homeless people on our streets is increasing, according to a Government report out today. Some argue that the homeless have only themselves to blame but other feel that ...

1.7 YEAR 8 FLASHBACK

Extract from *Holes* by Louis Sachar

Stanley's great-great-grandfather was named Elya Yelnats. He was born in Latvia. When he was fifteen years old he fell in love with Myra Menke.

(He didn't know he was Stanley's great-great-grandfather.)

Myra Menke was fourteen. She would turn fifteen in two months, at which time her father had decided she should be married.

Elya went to her father to ask for her hand, but so did Igor Barkov, the pig farmer. Igor was fifty-seven years old. He had a red nose and fat puffy cheeks.

'I will trade you my fattest pig for your daughter,' Igor offered.

'And what have you got?' Myra's father asked Elya.

'A heart full of love,' said Elya.

'I'd rather have a fat pig,' said Myra's father.

Desperate, Elya went to see Madame Zeroni, an old Egyptian woman who lived on the edge of town. He had become friends with her, though she was quite a bit older than him. She was even older than Igor Barkov.

The other boys of his village liked to mud wrestle. Elya preferred visiting Madame Zeroni and listening to her many stories.

Madame Zeroni had dark skin and a very wide mouth. When she looked at you, her eyes seemed to expand, and you felt like she was looking right through you.

'Elya, what's wrong?' she asked, before he even told her he was upset. She was sitting in a homemade wheelchair. She had no left foot. Her leg stopped at her ankle.

'I'm in love with Myra Menke,' Elya confessed. 'But Igor Barkov has offered to trade his fattest pig for her. I can't compete with that.'

'Good,' said Madame Zeroni. 'You're too young to get married. You've got your whole life ahead of you.'

'But I love Myra.'

'Myra's head is as empty as a flowerpot.'

'But she's beautiful.'

'So is a flowerpot. Can she push a plow? Can she milk a goat? No, she is too delicate. Can she have an intelligent conversation? No, she is silly and foolish. Will she take care of you when you are sick? No, she is spoiled and will only want you to take care of her. So, she is beautiful. So what? Ptuui!'

Madame Zeroni spat on the dirt.

She told Elya that he should go to America. 'Like my son. That's where your future lies. Not with Myra Menke.'

But Elya would hear none of that. He was fifteen, and all he could see was Myra's shallow beauty.

Madame Zeroni hated to see Elya so forlorn. Against her better judgment, she agreed to help him.

1.8 YEAR 9 MACBETH'S BANQUET

Summary of *Macbeth* Act 3 Scene 4, lines 1–110

- Macbeth and Lady Macbeth welcome their guests to a banquet.

- One of the murderers arrives and secretly tells Macbeth that Banquo has been killed but Fleance has escaped.

- Macbeth returns to the banquet and then claims to see Banquo's ghost, but no one else can see it.

- Lady Macbeth and the guests are upset and Lady Macbeth tries to cover up for Macbeth.

- Macbeth sees the ghost several times and finally Lady Macbeth asks the guests to leave.

 **1.9 YEAR 9 MACBETH'S BANQUET**

1 Fill in the thought bubbles for the characters in the picture below:

2 How do the characters feel at the end of the scene?
Draw lines to join up characters with their feelings.
Some characters may have more than one feeling or share the same feelings with another character.
Use a dictionary if you are unsure what the words mean.

Characters	Feelings
Macbeth	Disappointed
	Anxious
	Embarrassed
	Resentful
Lady Macbeth	Determined
	Guilty
	Surprised
Ross	Terrified
	Insecure
	Stressed
Lennox	Confused
	Uneasy
	Threatened
Lords and Attendants	Angry

1.10 YEAR 9   MACBETH'S BANQUET

A Lord's Diary

Complete the diary entry, using the space below:

FRIDAY

My wife and I have been invited to attend a banquet at Macbeth's castle

tomorrow night. It's quite an honour and we are looking forward to it.

SATURDAY

The banquet was disappointing. We had to leave early because . . .

_____

_____

_____

_____

_____

_____

_____

_____

_____

_____

_____

_____

_____

_____

1.11 YEAR 9 MACBETH MEETS THE WITCHES

Card 1

Card 2

'Beware the Thane of Fife. Dismiss me. Enough.'

Card 3

1.11 YEAR 9 MACBETH MEETS THE WITCHES

Card 4

'Be bloody, bold, and resolute; laugh to scorn / The power of man, for none of woman born / Shall harm Macbeth'

Card 5

Card 6

'Macbeth shall never vanquished be until Great Birnham Wood to high Dunsinane hill / Shall come against him'

2.1 YEAR 7 THE PIED PIPER

Writing a Biased View in Favour of the Mayor

Imagine the following:

You are a member of the Mayor of Hamelin's family.
The townspeople have created a sculpture to commemorate the lost children.
You have offered to write an inscription to go underneath the sculpture.
You want to use the inscription to persuade people that the Pied Piper and the townspeople were more to blame for the lost children than the Mayor.

> **Your task is to:**
>
> **Write an inscription of around 75 words for the sculpture depicted below.**
> **Make the inscription biased in favour of the Mayor.**

Here are some tips:
Write a rough draft on scrap paper first, then copy your final version into the box below the sculpture or onto a separate piece of paper. Mention the *main events* in the story but try to choose words that will make the readers think that the Mayor was NOT to blame.

2.2 YEAR 7 THE PIED PIPER

Choose sentences to go on an inscription for this sculpture.
Underline the sentence in each box which will make people think it was **the Mayor's fault** that the children disappeared. The first box has been done for you.

---

1 Hamelin town was full of rats but the poor Mayor didn't know what to do.
2 <u>Hamelin town was full of rats but the lazy Mayor did nothing until the people complained.</u>

---

1 The sly Mayor offered a reward to anyone who could rid the town of the rats, but he didn't really mean it.
2 The kind Mayor offered a reward to anyone who could rid the town of the rats.

---

1 A Pied Piper cleverly played his pipe and saved the town by leading the rats to the river to drown.
2 A Pied Piper needed the reward so he played his pipe and led the rats to the river to drown.

---

1 The Mayor was pleased but sadly could not afford to pay the Pied Piper, because he needed the money to help the poor people of the town.
2 The crafty Mayor knew that the rats would not return so he refused to pay the Pied Piper.

---

1 The Pied Piper wanted to teach the evil Mayor a lesson, so he played his pipe and led the children away to live in a better land inside the mountain.
2 The Pied Piper was angry with the poor Mayor, so he played his pipe and led the children away to live inside a dark mountain for ever.

YOUR OWN OPINION
Write here who *you* think was to blame for the loss of the children and why.

2.3a YEAR 8   FAMILY RELATIONSHIPS

Digging

Between my finger and my thumb
The squat pen rests: snug as a gun.

Under my window, a clean rasping sound
When the spade sinks into gravelly ground:
My father, digging. I look down

Till his straining rump among the flowerbeds
Bends low, comes up twenty years away
Stooping in rhythm through potato drills
Where he was digging.

The coarse boot nestled on the lug, the shaft
Against the inside knee was levered firmly.
He rooted out tall tops, buried the bright edge deep
To scatter new potatoes that we picked
Loving their cool hardness in our hands.

By God, the old man could handle a spade.
Just like his old man.

My grandfather cut more turf in a day
Than any other man on Toner's bog.
Once I carried him milk in a bottle
Corked sloppily with paper. He straightened up
To drink it, then fell to right away
Nicking and slicing neatly, heaving sods
Over his shoulder, going down and down
For the good turf. Digging.

The cold smell of potato mould, the squelch and slap
Of soggy peat, the curt cuts of an edge
Through living roots awaken in my head.
But I've no spade to follow men like them.

Between my finger and my thumb
The squat pen rests.
I'll dig with it.

Seamus Heaney

2.3b YEAR 8 FAMILY RELATIONSHIPS

My Hero

My dad's as brave as a dad can be,
I rate him Number One,
He's not afraid of the dead of night,
Or anything under the sun.

He's not afraid of a late-night film,
Full of horrors on the telly,
And is he afraid of skeletons?
Not dad, not on your Nelly!

He's not afraid of meeting ghosts,
He'd even smile and greet 'em,
And things that scare most dads the most,
My dad could just defeat 'em.

He's not afraid of vampires,
Or a wolf-man come to get him,
If Frankenstein's monster knocked on our door,
He wouldn't let that upset him.

My dad's as brave as a dad can be,
And he's always ready to prove it.
So why, when a spider's in the bath,
Does mum have to come and remove it?

Willis Hall

2.4a YEAR 8 FAMILY RELATIONSHIPS

Lullaby

Go to sleep, Mum,
I won't stop breathing
suddenly, in the night.

Go to sleep, I won't
climb out of my cot and
tumble downstairs.

Mum, I won't swallow
the pills the doctor gave you or
put hairpins in electric
sockets, just go to sleep.

I won't cry
when you take me to school and leave me:
I'll be happy with other children
my own age.

Sleep, Mum, sleep.
I won't
fall in the pond, play with matches,
run under a lorry or even consider
sweets from strangers.

No, I won't
give you a lot of lip,
not like some.

I won't sniff glue,
fail all my exams,
get myself/
my girlfriend pregnant.
I'll work hard and get a steady/
really worthwhile job.
I promise, go to sleep.

I'll never forget
to drop in/phone/write
and if
I need any milk, I'll yell.

Rosemary Norman

2.4b YEAR 8   FAMILY RELATIONSHIPS

Catrin

I can remember you, child,
As I stood in a hot, white
Room at the window watching
The people and cars taking
Turn at the traffic lights.
I can remember you, our first
Fierce confrontation, the tight
Red rope of love which we both
Fought over. It was a square
Environmental blank, disinfected
Of paintings or toys. I wrote
All over the walls with my
Words, coloured the clean squares
With the wild, tender circles
Of our struggle to become
Separate. We want, we shouted,
To be two, to be ourselves.

Neither won nor lost the struggle
In the glass tank clouded with feelings
Which changed us both. Still I am fighting
You off, as you stand there
With your straight, strong, long
Brown hair and your rosy,
Defiant glare, bringing up
From the heart's pool that old rope,
Tightening about my life,
Trailing love and conflict,
As you ask may you skate
In the dark, for one more hour.

Gillian Clarke

Poem

And if it snowed and snow covered the drive
he took a spade and tossed it to one side.
And always tucked his daughter up at night.
And slippered her the one time that she lied.

And every week he tipped up half his wage.
And what he didn't spend each week he saved.
And praised his wife for every meal she made.
And once, for laughing, punched her in the face.

And for his mum he hired a private nurse.
And every Sunday taxied her to church.
And he blubbed when she went from bad to worse.
And twice he lifted ten quid from her purse.

Here's how they rated him when they looked back:
sometimes he did this, sometimes he did that.

Simon Armitage

3.1 YEAR 7 SHOULD WE BAN ZOOS?

The plus sign indicates that this is an argument *for* keeping zoos.

1+   Zoos can educate people about wild animals.

2+   Zoos keep animals safe from being attacked by other animals.

3+   Zoos can save rare animals from becoming extinct.

4+   Many people would never see wild animals if it wasn't for zoos.

5+   Zoos are popular and people will continue to pay to visit them.

6+   Wild animals don't think like humans and so they don't feel degraded living in zoos.

The minus sign indicates that this is an argument *against* keeping zoos.

7–   Zoos are too expensive to run.

8–   Wild animals can become stressed if they are kept in small spaces.

9–   People can learn more about animals from books, videos and TV than from zoos.

10–   Most animals have natural ways of protecting themselves from attack and don't need zoos.

11–   Rare animals can be saved by protecting them in their natural habitat, rather than in zoos.

12–   It is cruel to keep animals in unnatural conditions like zoos.

13–   Zoos are degrading for animals.

14–   Zoos prevent wild animals from living a natural life.

3.2 YEAR 8 BOOKS VERSUS COMPUTERS

The plus sign indicates that this is a point in favour of books.

1+	Books are lighter and easier to move around than computers.
2+	Books can be read without the need for a screen or table.
3+	Books have more room for pictures and other illustrations than computer screens.
4+	Books do not need any hardware.
5+	Books are cheaper to buy than computers.
6+	It is easier to read novels and longer texts in book form than on computer screens.
7+	Books are more reliable than computers, which can go wrong.

The minus sign indicates that this is a point in favour of computers.

8−	Finding information on a computer is easier and quicker than searching through books.
9−	You can access a wide range of up-to-date information on a computer.
10−	Most computers can be linked to other communication systems such as email and the Internet.
11−	Computers can access sound and high-quality images, including moving images.
12−	Computers last longer than books because they do not become damaged through wear and tear.
13−	Computers are attractive to young people and will encourage them to read more.
14−	More computers in libraries will encourage more people to use the libraries.

3.3 YEAR 9 VERDICT ON THE MEDIA

Is the Media Guilty of Misconduct?

The plus sign indicates that the point is in favour of the media.

1+	The media helps solve crime through publicity.
2+	The media educates people in their own homes.
3+	The media provides company and entertainment for housebound people.
4+	The media helps the economy by providing jobs and encouraging people to buy things.
5+	The media provides good publicity for charities and good causes.
6+	Undercover documentaries protect the public through uncovering fraud and crime.
7+	The media entertains young people and keeps them off the streets.

The minus sign indicates that the point is NOT in favour of the media.

8–	Reporting crime in the media frightens people, particularly children and the elderly.
9–	Violent films and videos make some people more violent.
10–	The media is too powerful and can destroy people's lives.
11–	The news only concentrates on bad events, and makes people feel depressed about the world.
12–	Adverts in the media make people dissatisfied with their lives.
13–	The media is only interested in sensationalism and rarely reports the truth.
14–	Unrealistic images of perfect people in the media create eating disorders and low self-esteem.

4.1 **YEAR 7** **THE PUNCTUATION CHALLENGE**

After two days as evacuees we ran away

We thumbed a lift and then walked the rest of the way home

My Gran opened the door and nearly fainted

4.2 YEAR 7 THE PUNCTUATION CHALLENGE

What are you two doing here

she said

Your Mum will kill you

4.3 YEAR 7 THE PUNCTUATION CHALLENGE

1 Put in the missing punctuation marks:

After two days as evacuees we ran away We thumbed a lift and then walked the rest of the way home My Gran opened the door and nearly fainted What are you two doing here she said Your Mum will kill you

2 Put in the missing punctuation marks:

He turned to Spurling who was standing beside him Have you poured me a brandy Spurling

Yes Sir Hubert

Well you can drink it for me too I haven't got time

Taking the glass the chauffeur bowed and left the room

From *The Switch* by Anthony Horowitz

4.4 YEAR 7   THE PUNCTUATION CHALLENGE

He turned to Spurling

who was standing beside him

Have you poured me a brandy Spurling

Yes

Sir Hubert

Well you can drink it for me too

I haven't got time

Taking the glass the chauffeur bowed and left the room

4.6 YEAR 8   MIDSUMMER DREAM

Extract from *A Midsummer Night's Dream* Act 2 Scene 1 by William Shakespeare

In this part of the play, King Oberon and Queen Titania meet each other unexpectedly and both jump to the conclusion that the other is there in Athens to bless the wedding of a former lover. In this extract, Titania blames Oberon for their quarrelling and adds that this has brought about severe problems and unnatural changes in the seasons, such as flooding, rotting crops, summer weather in winter and winter weather in summer.

1 *Titania*: These are the <u>forgeries</u> of <u>jealousy;</u>
2 And <u>never</u> since the <u>middle summer's spring</u>
3 <u>Met</u> we on <u>hill</u>, in <u>dale</u>, <u>forest,</u> or <u>mead</u>,
4 By <u>paved fountain</u> or by <u>rushy brook</u>,
5 Or in the <u>beached margent of the sea</u>
6 To <u>dance</u> our <u>ringlets</u> to the <u>whistling wind</u>,
7 But with thy <u>brawls</u> thou hast <u>disturbed</u> our <u>sport.</u>
8 Therefore the <u>winds</u>, <u>piping</u> to us <u>in vain</u>,
9 As in <u>revenge</u> have <u>sucked up</u> from the <u>sea</u>
10 <u>Contagious fogs</u> which, <u>falling</u> in the <u>land</u>,
11 Hath every <u>pelting river</u> made so <u>proud</u>
12 That they have <u>overborne</u> their <u>continents.</u>
13 The <u>ox</u> hath therefore <u>stretch'd</u> his <u>yoke in vain</u>,
14 The <u>ploughman</u> <u>lost his sweat</u>, and the green <u>corn</u>
15 Hath <u>rotted</u> <u>ere</u> his <u>youth</u> <u>attained a beard.</u>
16 The <u>fold</u> stands <u>empty</u> in the <u>drowned field</u>,
17 And <u>crows</u> are <u>fatted</u> with the <u>murrion flock</u>.
18 The <u>nine men's morris</u> is <u>filled up</u> with <u>mud</u>,
19 And the <u>quaint mazes</u> in the <u>wanton green</u>,
20 For lack of <u>tread</u> are <u>indistinguishable.</u>
20 The <u>human mortals</u> <u>want their winter</u> cheer.
22 No <u>night</u> is now with <u>hymn or carol blessed.</u>
23 Therefore the <u>moon</u>, the <u>governess</u> of <u>floods</u>,
24 Pale in her <u>anger washes</u> all the <u>air</u>,
25 That <u>rheumatic diseases</u> <u>do abound;</u>
26 And <u>thorough</u> this <u>distemperature</u> we <u>see</u>
27 The <u>seasons</u> alter: <u>hoary-headed frosts</u>
28 <u>Fall</u> in <u>the fresh lap of the crimson rose</u>,
29 And on <u>old Hiems'</u> <u>thin</u> and <u>icy crown</u>
30 An <u>odorous chaplet</u> of <u>sweet summer buds</u>
31 Is, as in <u>mock'ry</u>, set. The <u>spring</u>, the <u>summer</u>,
32 The <u>childing autumn</u>, <u>angry winter</u> change
33 Their <u>wonted liveries</u>, and the <u>mazed world</u>
34 By their <u>increase</u> now knows not which is which.
35 And this same <u>progeny</u> of <u>evils</u> comes
36 From our <u>debate</u>, from our <u>dissension.</u>
37 We are their <u>parents</u> and <u>original</u>.

4.7a YEAR 8 MIDSUMMER DREAM

Use these definitions to help you create a movement or action for each of the underlined words or phrases in *your* part of the poem.

Forgeries – a copy made for a dishonest purpose

Jealousy – the emotion of envy or possessiveness

Middle summer's spring – early summer

Dale – a valley

Mead – a meadow, or a low-lying field of grass used for grazing animals

Paved fountain – a water spring with a pebbled bed

Rushy – covered in rushes or stalklike plants found near marshes; linked also to the word rush, meaning to hurry, when used to describe fast-moving water

Brook – a small stream

Beached margent of the sea – a sandy stretch of seashore

Ringlet – a pattern of rings made by fairies dancing in a circle

Brawls – a noisy quarrel or a fight

Disturbed – to interrupt or upset someone

Sport – used here to refer to general activities

Piping – the passage of air moving as through pipes, like a musical instrument

In vain – without success

Revenge – inflicting harm in return for an injury or wrong received (getting your own back)

Sucked up – drawn in by suction, like liquid through a straw

Contagious fogs – fogs that spread easily from one object to another, like an infectious disease

Pelting – likely to be linked to the word 'paltry', which means insignificant, small or trivial

Proud – used here this means overflowing or raised above the surrounding surface

Overborne – overflowed by becoming too powerful

Continents – land mass; used here it refers to the river banks

Yoke – a wooden frame put over the necks of oxen to keep them together when pulling a plough

Lost his sweat – worked for nothing or for no result

4.7b YEAR 8 MIDSUMMER DREAM

Ere – before

Attained a beard – grew a beard

Fold – an enclosed fenced area for sheep or cattle

Murrion flock – sheep killed by a disease called murrain that only affects cattle

Nine men's morris – a game played outside on 3 squares, with 9 pins on each side, with the aim to get 3 pins in a row

Quaint mazes – an old-fashioned maze; used here it refers to labyrinths of paths kept in good condition by people running along them

Wanton green – greenery allowed to grow wild

Want their winter – miss their usual winter

Blessed – meaning to have an advantage or have something good happen to you

Governess – a teacher in authority or control

Washes – used here this word means to fill with moisture

Rheumatic diseases – diseases of the joints

Do abound – exist in large numbers

Thorough – through

Distemperature – upsetting of the weather

Hoary – white or grey with age

The fresh lap of the crimson rose – a way of saying 'in summer'

Old Hiems – a way of referring to winter

Thin – used here this word means bald

Odorous chaplet – a perfumed wreath of flowers worn on the head

Childing – producing fruit

Wonted liveries – usual appearance

Mazed – puzzled

Progeny of evils – child of or result of evil

Debate – quarrel

Dissension – disagreement

Original – origin or beginning

4.8 YEAR 9 SHAKESPEARE – THE SILENT MOVIE

Summary of *Twelfth Night* Act 1 by William Shakespeare

SCENE 1   *At Orsino's house*   *Enter Orsino, duke of Illyria, Curio and other lords*
Duke Orsino listens to music to take his mind off his love for Lady Olivia.
A servant called Valentine arrives to tell Orsino that Olivia is still mourning the death of her brother and will not meet with anyone.
Orsino is very upset and everyone leaves the stage.

SCENE 2   *On a seashore*   *Enter Viola, a Captain and sailors*
Viola and a Captain arrive after surviving a shipwreck, in which Viola became separated from her identical twin brother, Sebastian.
The captain tells Viola about Orsino and his love for Olivia. Viola finds a trunk of clothes belonging to her brother and decides to dress up as a man in order to obtain a job at Orsino's court. Everyone leaves the stage.

SCENE 3   *At Olivia's house*   *Enter Sir Toby Belch and Maria*
Sir Toby Belch, Olivia's uncle, tells Maria how angry he is at Olivia's decision to remain in mourning, because he wants her to marry his friend, Sir Andrew Aguecheek.

Enter Andrew Aguecheek
Maria has a conversation with Andrew Aguecheek that reveals he is not very clever and then she leaves. Andrew Aguecheek tells Sir Toby that he is not confident that Olivia will agree to meet him, but Sir Toby persuades him to stay another month and they go off to have a drinking session.

SCENE 4   *At Orsino's house*   *Enter Valentine, Orsino's servant, and Viola dressed as a man*
Viola (now calling herself Cesario) has been working as Orsino's messenger for 3 days. Valentine tells Cesario that he has impressed Orsino.

Enter Orsino, Curio, and attendants
Orsino sends Cesario to Olivia with a message of love and a request to meet her. However, Cesario finds that she is falling in love with Orsino. Everyone leaves the stage.

SCENE 5   *At Olivia's house*   *Enter Maria and Feste the Clown*
Maria tries to persuade Feste to tell her where he has been, but he refuses and Maria leaves.

Enter Olivia with Malvolio and attendants
Olivia wants to send Feste away, but they have a lighthearted conversation until Maria enters, announcing the arrival of Cesario. Whilst Olivia decided whether to let Cesario in, Sir Toby arrives in a state of drunkenness and then leaves.
Olivia lets Cesario in and finds that she enjoys his company.
When Cesario leaves, she sends her steward Malvolio after him with a ring that she pretends he has left behind and tells Malvolio to ask him to return tomorrow.

6.1a YEAR 7 STORY SETTINGS

Extract from *The Hobbit* by J.R.R. Tolkien

An unexpected party

In a hole in the ground there lived a hobbit. Not a nasty, dirty, wet hole, filled with the ends of worms and an oozy smell, nor yet a dry, bare, sandy hole with nothing in it to sit down on or to eat: it was a hobbit-hole, and that means comfort.

It had a perfectly round door like a porthole, painted green, with a shiny yellow brass knob in the exact middle. The door opened on to a tube-shaped hall like a tunnel: a very comfortable tunnel without smoke, with panelled walls, and floors tiled and carpeted, provided with polished chairs, and lots and lots of pegs for hats and coats – the hobbit was fond of visitors. The tunnel wound on and on, going fairly but not quite straight into the side of the hill – The Hill, as all the people for many miles round called it – and many little round doors opened out of it, first on one side and then on another. No going upstairs for the hobbit: bedrooms, bathrooms, cellars, pantries (lots of these), wardrobes (he had whole rooms devoted to clothes), kitchens, dining-rooms, all were on the same floor, and indeed on the same passage. The best rooms were all on the lefthand side (going in), for these were the only ones to have windows, deep-set round windows looking over his garden, and meadows beyond, sloping down to the river.

This hobbit was a very well-to-do hobbit, and his name was Baggins. The Bagginses had lived in the neighbourhood of The Hill for time out of mind, and people considered them very respectable, not only because most of them were rich, but also because they never had any adventures or did anything unexpected . . .

6.1b YEAR 7   STORY SETTINGS

Extract from *Holes* by Louis Sachar

There is no lake at Camp Green Lake. There once was a very large lake here, the largest lake in Texas. That was over a hundred years ago. Now it is just a dry, flat wasteland.

There used to be a town of Green Lake as well. The town shriveled and dried up along with the lake, and the people who lived there.

During the summer the daytime temperature hovers around ninety-five degrees in the shade – if you can find any shade. There's not much shade in a big dry lake.

The only trees are two old oaks on the eastern edge of the 'lake.' A hammock is stretched between the two trees, and a log cabin stands behind that.

The campers are forbidden to lie in the hammock. It belongs to the Warden. The Warden owns the shade.

Out on the lake, rattlesnakes and scorpions find shade under rocks and in the holes dug by the campers.

6.1c   YEAR 7   STORY SETTINGS

Extract from *The Village Dinosaur* by Phyllis Arkle

Discovery in a chalk-pit

'What's going on?'
   'Something exciting!'
'Where?'
'Down at the old quarry.'
The news flashed through the village and shopkeepers locked up their shops and ran. Housewives rushed out of their houses without even bothering to bolt the doors.

Jed Watkins raced along – as usual, well behind the other boys – down the narrow, muddy, rutted lane leading to the disused chalk-pit. He could smell wood burning. Whatever could have happened? It was at a time like this that he wished he wasn't so much smaller than other boys of his age. He couldn't run as fast and he was always last on the scene.

When, panting, he arrived at the pit, most of the villagers were already there and two . . .

6.1d YEAR 7 STORY SETTINGS

Extract from *Playing on the Edge* by Neil Arksey

Level Playing Field

The adverts ended.

'Don't forget, tonight on BBC Sport, *Goalarama:* coverage of the monster clash: Gunman Reds versus Blue City Rangers. No doubt about it – it's going to be a thrill-a-minute match. But twice the excitement when you watch it here, with us.

'Yes, once again, we'll be on the pitch with the players. Exclusive access to all player-to-player and manager-to-player communications. The BBC's unique epaulette micro-cameras bringing you player-point-of-view shots at all the critical moments, throughout the game. *Plus* press-of-a-button interactive action replay. *You* call the shots!

'There will, of course, be unrivalled commentary: the usual suspects down at Highbury, and big-name guests here in the studio, watching the game and sharing their views with us in our post-match analysis.

'It's going to be one stupendous night of football action. There's only one place to be: *Goalarama* . . . on the BBC.'

*

Towering above Highbury Fields, the Gunman Reds' stadium gleamed in the sunlight.

Easy swerved, slipped past the first defender and accelerated inside the second. He glanced back. Heads jerking, arms, and legs pumping, players thundered behind. No chance of support – his nearest teammate was way back. Any waiting around and the advantage would be lost.

'Go for it!'

'Go*waan*, Easy – do the business!'

Had they been playing on a pitch, with lines and goal posts and everything, he'd be inside the penalty area by now. Closing fast from an angle, he skipped a high tackle, barged between the last two defenders and charged towards a pile of bags and jackets – the nearside post.

The keeper came out low, spreading wide his big gloved hands.

Easy changed tack, dancing the ball, searching for a way past. The keeper scowled. Easy dummied a lob. The keeper sprang, too late he saw the trap and tried to check his flight – Easy's ball, gently toe-poked, was through his legs and over the line.

'Naaaaah!'

'Yeeeees!'

Game over. Easy cartwheeled and ran towards the onlookers.

'*Easy! Easy!*' Trix, his younger sister and proudest, most loyal fan, proclaimed her delight. 'Way to go, bro!'

6.2 YEAR 7 STORY SETTINGS

What did the character see?
(make a quick sketch)

What else did the character sense?
(i.e. hear, feel, smell, taste)
(write single words or short phrases)

What emotions did the character feel and/or what did he/she think about?
(write single words or short phrases such as *he/she felt as if . . .; it reminded him/her of . . .*)

How did the character react?
(write single words or short phrases)

6.3 YEAR 8 ILLNESS IN THE FAMILY

Extract from *About Face* by Paul Whitfield

(Light up to reveal *Rachel*, centre front, and friends.)

SAMANTHA

You coming out tonight, Rachel?

EMMA

Why don't you ever come out?

BILL

You won't have any friends left.

HAYLEY

How's your Mum, Rachel?

SAMANTHA

Can I come round to yours?

EMMA

Why doesn't anyone ever go round to yours?

JOE

What's up with your Mum?

AMY

Saw your Mum the other day.

BILL

What's up with her, Rachel?

DEAN

She's right weird.

AMY

She's weird, your Mum is.

6.4 YEAR 8 ILLNESS IN THE FAMILY

Harry Pushed Her

Harry pushed her;
He pushed her around;
He pushed his sister.
Before school, after school;
On weekends.
He pushed his sister;
He had no friends.
He pushed her – school-holidays
And Christmas time.
The children always
Sang their made-up rhyme:
'Harry push her, push her now!
Harry push the crazy cow!'
Harry pushed her without strain:
Through snow, sunshine, wind and rain.
She smiled strangely
And never said a word.
He pushed her for years –
It was so absurd.
Harry was twelve;
His sister twenty-three.
Harry never had a childhood like me.
Harry pushed her without a care;
He pushed his sister in her wheelchair.

Peter Thabit Jones

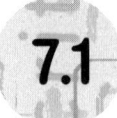

7.1 YEAR 7 WRITING PLAYS

Checklist for Writing Plays

- The writing is split up into scenes.

- Each scene begins with a list of characters and an exact description of the set.

- The names of characters are usually written down the left-hand side.

- Plays do not use speech marks, or the word *said* when characters speak.

- Each new speech is set out on a new line and begins with a capital letter.

- Stage directions and sound effects are in brackets.

- Stage directions are written in the present tense

  e.g. (*Joel sits next to Kate*).

- Special terms are used for some stage directions e.g. *off stage*, *aside*.

- Occasionally instructions in brackets tell actors how to say certain lines:

  e.g. KATE (*Whispering to Joel*) Does he know we've met before?

- Contrast can be used to build tension, for example:

  a) moments of silence placed within conversation make scenes more interesting by creating tension between characters

  b) pleasant or amusing sections placed between sad or tragic sections of a play make the tragic parts seem even more tragic.

7.2 YEAR 7 THE BRADLEY PAINTING CHALLENGE

First prize   Painting Number 314
'The old house'
By Mr Joseph Purnell

Second prize   Painting Number 259
'The town'
By Ms Kate Harrison

Third prize   Painting Number 166
'The park'
By Lady Joan Lancaster

7.3 YEAR 9 VERSIONS OF THE PARDONER'S TALE

Extract from *The Canterbury Tales* by Geraldine McCaughrean

Death's Murderers

The man Snatch was slumped over a table at the Tabard Inn in Southwark – (you may know the place). He had wetted his brain in beer, and it weighed heavy. The clanging of the church bell registered dully in his ears. 'Who are they burying?' he asked.

Old Harry, the landlord, who was wiping tables close by, said, 'Don't you know? I wondered why you weren't at the funeral – him being a friend of yours. It's Colley the Fence. Caught it last Wednesday and gone today. Him and his wife and his two boys.'

'Caught what?' demanded Snatch, grasping Harry's arm.

'The Black Death, of course!'

Then another customer chimed in. 'Ay, they do say the Plague came to Combleton over yonder, and Death laid hands on every man, woman and child and carried 'em off.'

'Where? Carried them off where?' demanded Snatch, fighting his way through drink-haze like a ghost through cobwebs.

'Who knows where Death carries men off to,' said a deeply hooded character sitting in the corner of the bar, 'but he sure enough comes for every man in the end. And he's taken twice his share recently, thanks to the Plague.'

Tears of indignation started into Snatch's eyes. 'I don't see what gives Death the right to go carrying off anyone!' he slurred. 'And if you ask me, it's about time some brave soul stood up to Death and put an end to his carryings-on – his carryings-off I mean. Dip! Cut! Where are you?' And he stumbled off into the sunlight to look for his two closest friends.

Dip was at home in bed, but not for long. Snatch knocked him up and called him into the street. They met with Cut coming home from a card-game and cursing his empty pockets.

Snatch threw an arm over each friend's shoulder. 'Have you heard? Old Colley the Fence is dead. Death carried off him and all his family in a couple of days. Let's take an oath, friends, not to rest until we've tracked down this "Death" fellow and stuck a knife between his ribs. Think what the mayor and parish would pay if we brought in Death's dead body. Besides – how many purses do you think he's emptied on the dark highway, eh? Death must have made himself quite a walletful by now.'

Cut fingered his sharp penknife – the one he used for cutting purses. Dip felt his fingers itch at the promise of rich pickings. 'We're with you, neighbour Snatch!' they cried, and off they reeled, not the sum total of one brain between the three of them.

7.4a YEAR 9 VERSIONS OF THE PARDONER'S TALE

Extract from a modern translation of Geoffrey Chaucer's *The Canterbury Tales* by Nevill Coghill

The Pardoner's Tale

It's of three rioters I have to tell
Who, long before the morning service bell,
Were sitting in a tavern for a drink.
And as they sat, they heard the hand-bell clink
Before a coffin going to the grave;
One of them called the little tavern-knave
And said 'Go and find out at once – look spry! –
Whose corpse is in that coffin passing by;
And see you get the name correctly too.'
'Sir,' said the boy, 'no need, I promise you;
Two hours before you came here I was told.
He was a friend of yours in days of old,
And suddenly, last night, the man was slain,
Upon his bench, face up, dead drunk again.
There came a privy thief, they call him Death,
Who kills us all round here, and in a breath
He speared him through the heart, he never stirred.
And then Death went his way without a word.
He's killed a thousand in the present plague,
And, sir, it doesn't do to be too vague
If you should meet him; you had best be wary.
Be on your guard with such an adversary,
Be primed to meet him everywhere you go,
That's what my mother said. It's all I know.'

7.4b YEAR 9 VERSIONS OF THE PARDONER'S TALE

Continued extract from a modern translation of Geoffrey Chaucer's *The Canterbury Tales* by Nevill Coghill

The publican joined in with, 'By St Mary,
What the child says is right; you'd best be wary,
This very year he killed, in a large village
A mile away, man, woman, serf at tillage.
Page in the household, children – all there were.
Yes, I imagine that he lives round there.
It's well to be prepared in these alarms,
He might do you dishonour.' 'Huh, God's arms!'
    The rioter said, 'Is he so fierce to meet?
I'll search for him, by Jesus, street by street.
God's blessed bones! I'll register a vow!
Here, chaps! The three of us together now,
Hold up your hands, like me, and we'll be brothers
In this affair, and each defend the others,
And we will kill this traitor Death, I say!
Away with him as he has made away
With all our friends. God's dignity! Tonight!'
    They made their bargain, swore with appetite,
These three, to live and die for one another
As brother-born might swear to his born brother.
And up they started in their drunken rage
And made towards this village which the page
And publican had spoken of before.
Many and grisly were the oaths they swore,
Tearing Christ's blessed body to a shred;
'If we can only catch him, Death is dead!'

7.4c YEAR 9 VERSIONS OF THE PARDONER'S TALE

Extract from *The Pardoner's Tale* by Geoffrey Chaucer

Thise riotoures thre of whiche I telle,
Longe erst er prime rong of any belle,
Were set hem in a taverne for to drinke,
And as they sat, they herde a belle clinke
Biforn a cors, was caried to his grave.
That oon of hem gan callen to his knave:
'Go bet,' quod he, 'and axe redily
What cors is this that passeth heer forby;
And looke that thou reporte his name weel.'
    'Sire,' quod this boy, 'it nedeth never-a-deel;
It was me toold er ye cam heer two houres.
He was, pardee, an old felawe of youres;
And sodeynly he was yslain to-night,
Fordronke, as he sat on his bench upright.
Ther cam a privee theef men clepeth Deeth,
That in this contree al the peple sleeth,
And with his spere he smoot his herte atwo,
And wente his wey withouten wordes mo.
He hath a thousand slain this pestilence.
And, maister, er ye come in his presence,
Me thinketh that it were necessarie
For to be war of swich an adversarie.
Beth redy for to meete him everemoore;
Thus taughte me my dame; I sey namoore.'
'By seinte Marie,' seyde this taverner,
'The child seith sooth, for he hath slain this yeer,
Henne over a mile, withinne a greet village,
Bothe man and womman, child, and hine, and page;

I trowe his habitacioun be there.
To been avised greet wisdom it were,
Er that he dide a man a dishonour.'
    'Ye, Goddes armes!' quod this riotour,
'Is it swich peril with him for to meete?
I shal him seke by wey and eek by strete,
I make avow to Goddes digne bones!
Herkneth, felawes, we thre been al ones;
Lat ech of us holde up his hand til oother,
And ech of us bicomen otheres brother,
And we wol sleen this false traitour Deeth.
He shal be slain, he that so manye sleeth,
By Goddes dignitee, er it be night.'
    Togidres han thise thre hir trouthes plight
To live and dien ech of hem for oother,
As though he were his owene ybore brother.
And up they stirte, al dronken in this rage,
And forth they goon towardes that village
Of which the taverner hadde spoke biforn.
And many a grisly ooth thanne han they sworn,
And Cristes blessed body al torente—
Deeth shal be deed, if that they may him hente.

7.5a YEAR 9   VERSIONS OF THE PARDONER'S TALE

Extract from *Dicing with Death* by Simon Adorian

(Solemn music and slow drumbeat. The CROWD falls silent.
Four COFFIN BEARERS walk past the stage, carrying a coffin.)

HARRY	Oy!
COFFIN BEARER	Sir?
HARRY	Who've you got there, then?
COFFIN BEARER	Perhaps you would know, if you had not spent your day dicing.
JAKE	Watch your tongue, man. We'll have you know we haven't just spent our day dicing. We've been drinking as well!
	(WALLY breaks wind loudly.)
WALLY	Better out than in.
HARRY & JAKE	*(Fanning the air around their noses.)* Urgggh, Wally!
WALLY	Sorry, boys.
HARRY	Listen, pal, just tell us who you're burying. We don't need any advice on how to live from you with your face as long as a wet Sunday.
COFFIN BEARER	It looks as if you are in need of plenty of advice. As the Book tells us, *The wages of sin is death.* Once there were four dicers, now there are but three. *(To the other COFFIN BEARERS.)* Move on.
	(Funeral procession leaves, drum beating slowly.)
	(HARRY, WALLY and JAKE stare at the empty chair in stunned silence.)
HARRY	It must have been . . .
JAKE	No wonder he was late for the game.
WALLY	And he owed me money.
HARRY	Shut up! This is no joking matter.
WALLY & JAKE	Sorry, Haz.
HARRY	We've got to do something to avenge our mate.
WALLY & JAKE	Revenge!
HARRY	But first, we gotta find out who it was who killed him.
WALLY & JAKE	Ah! Good plan, good plan.
HARRY	You boy!
	(SERVANT comes over to the table.)
HARRY	Were you aware of this . . . er . . . inconvenience to our business partner?
SERVANT	The whole village has talked about nothing else for the past day, sir.
	(WALLY collapses face down on the table. JAKE puts a bottle to his mouth.)
HARRY	So how come we didn't know?
	(SERVANT looks at the table where WALLY is snoring and JAKE is slurping loudly.)
SERVANT	I can't imagine, sir.
JAKE	*(Leaping up and staggering around the stage.)* So who killed him? 'Cos, whoever it is, he'd better watch out! Just give us his name.
	(Long pause. WALLY snores on.)
SERVANT	His name . . .
HARRY & JAKE	Yes?
SERVANT	. . . is Death.
	(WALLY wakes with a start. HARRY and JAKE look alarmed.)
SERVANT	A sly thief, he is. Broke into your mate's house in the dead of night and caught 'im in his sleep, just as 'e was, drunk as a skunk, so 'e never knew a thing about it. Stole up on 'im and stabbed 'im through the heart.

7.5b YEAR 9 VERSIONS OF THE PARDONER'S TALE

Continued extract from *Dicing with Death* by Simon Adorian

WALLY	The dirty, lowlife scumbag!
SERVANT	He's a dangerous customer, make no mistake. During this recent plague, he must've done away with a thousand folk round these parts. You want to be on your guard against this Death bloke. *(LANDLORD comes over.)*
LANDLORD	The boy's right, I tell you. You should see what this Death has done in the next town, only a couple of miles from here.
JAKE	What's that, then?
LANDLORD	Only gone and killed every man, woman, child and serf in the place, that's all. I wouldn't be surprised if he wasn't still out that way. But he's not someone you'd want to meet.
HARRY	You reckon? You think we're scared?
JAKE	Us? Scared of Death? Huh! We're hard, we are.
WALLY	Rock hard.
HARRY	I'll go through the town street by street till I catch up with him.
JAKE	Me too.
WALLY	And me.
HARRY	And I swear by God's bones, we'll track him down and then we'll have him.
WALLY & JAKE	Yeah!
HARRY	Listen, boys. Wally, Jake, hold up your hands and swear we're in this together, and together we'll kill this traitor Death who's done in so many of our countrymen. Yes?
WALLY & JAKE	We swear.
WALLY	Just let us find him and he's dead.
JAKE	Death is dead! *(HARRY, WALLY and JAKE arm themselves with whatever is available – a broomstick, dustbin lid, clubs, etc. As they do so, they take up JAKE's chant. They start to leave.)*
HARRY, WALLY & JAKE	Death is dead!
LANDLORD	One moment, gentlemen. Your bill?
HARRY	You talk of the bill at a time like this? We're off on a heroic quest to slay the evil foe Death and you quibble over a few measly pence on the slate?
LANDLORD	But, but . . .
WALLY	Shame on you, sir.
JAKE	Petty, money-grubbing cheapskate!
HARRY	Out of our way! We'll settle up with you when we return. But first we have a score to settle with Death! *(The CROWD cheers as HARRY, WALLY and JAKE set off, chanting as they go.)*
HARRY, WALLY & JAKE	Death is dead! Death is dead! Death is dead!

8.1 YEARS 7, 8 & 9   PERFORMANCE

Eight Tips for Using the Voice on Stage

- Use pauses and slow down. Pause slightly after each sentence.

- Avoid speaking too softly but do not shout.

- *Slightly* exaggerate the emotions but be careful not to over act.

- Do not talk at the same level or pitch all the time. Vary your voice.

- If you are standing, keep your weight on both feet and stand tall.

- For speech-type lines, walk onto the stage and stop before you speak.

- When talking to the audience, make eye contact with them before you speak.

- If you make a mistake forget it and carry on – the audience may not notice.

8.2 YEARS 7, 8 & 9 EVALUATION

Evaluation Guide

Title of performance

Name of performing group or theatre company

Date and venue of performance

1 In your opinion, what was the most effective part of the performance and why?

2 In your opinion, what was the least effective part of the performance and why?

3 Did the audience appear to enjoy the whole performance, just parts of the performance or very little?

4 In your opinion, did the writer succeed in providing an interesting plot? Comment on what you liked best about the plot and what you liked least. Give reasons.

5 Describe any part of the plot that made you want to know what happened next.

6 Describe any part of the plot that made you think more deeply about something.

7 Describe any part of the performance that you found emotionally moving.

8 Make comments on the quality of the directing.
   Include your opinion on *some* of the following in your comments:
   • the set and the lighting
   • the costumes and the props
   • the way atmosphere was created through music and/or special effects
   • the way the actors portrayed the characters
   • the timing of important lines or moves
   • the use of tension in the relationships between the characters.

9 Would you recommend this performance to a friend? Give reasons.

9.1 YEAR 8 MRS CANNING'S CHALLENGE

Independent Age Support (Helping the aged to help themselves)

Customer profile

Mrs Canning, aged 84, currently living alone. Mrs Canning owns a dog which provides her with essential company and protection. However, her dog is in need of a life-saving operation and Mrs Canning cannot afford to pay the vet's fee.

Outline of Task

Mrs Canning has decided to sell some of her possessions to raise money for the dog to have the operation, but she needs some advice on drafting the adverts. Unfortunately, her possessions are of little value but according to our policy of helping the aged to help themselves, I have accepted the task in order that she may raise money for her dog herself.

Due to the challenging nature of this task, I have provided two examples (see below) illustrating how her possessions could be advertised without being dishonest. Please be aware of the need to use as few words as possible to keep the cost of the adverts down. A list of items for sale is enclosed with this task sheet.

Time Scale

Due to the urgent nature of the dog's operation we would need the adverts completed as soon as possible.

Thankyou for your co-operation.

J Purnell

Independent Age Support Co-ordinator

Examples of wording

Item one

A cheap, old fashioned hi-fi. The owner has had this a long time but never uses it.

The advert:

Midi hi-fi, twin tape, turntable. Good condition, hardly used. Bargain at £20
Tel: Blecksley 0066 7489

Item two

An old discoloured cream plastic alarm clock trimmed with gold. It has not worked for years.

The advert:

Retro style 1960s alarm clock with gold trim. Needs some repair. A potential antique. Good investment at £15 Tel: Blecksley 0066 7489

9.2 YEAR 8 MRS CANNING'S CHALLENGE

Independent Age Support (Helping the aged to help themselves)

List of items to be Advertised for Mrs Canning

- Two small brass candlesticks, one with some scratches on the base. Requested to sell at £10.

- One large round wall mirror in a dark brown wooden frame with a few faint green paint marks on one side. Requested to sell at £20.

- A man's inexpensive silver-coloured watch with broken black leather strap. Still works when wound up but tends to lose time. Requested to sell at £30.

- A patterned brass bangle in need of cleaning. Requested to sell at £10.

- A tall standing chrome birdcage. A present costing £100 three years ago but now in poor condition. Requested to sell at £50.

- Empty fish tank in antique pine cabinet with broken ornamental pump and faulty lights. Cost £150 when new several years ago. Requested to sell at £75.

- Flowered single quilt cover, with matching lamp shade. Quilt cover is faded and has been repaired at the seam. Lamp shade also faded. Requested to sell at £15.

- White 14-inch remote control portable black and white TV. Grubby appearance. Request to sell at £15.

9.3 YEAR 9 LIVING WITH MENTAL ILLNESS

Dear *Kudos,*

Please can you advise me on what to do. I have never written to a magazine before and feel stupid but I don't know where else to turn. This is my story.

I am 14 years old and I have a sister who is 2 years younger than me. She is mentally disabled. She can be funny and laughs at all sorts of things but she can suddenly turn aggressive and start to swear really loudly for nothing. We try to ignore her at home but she can hurt people when she grabs hold of their arm or hits them and once someone complained about her swearing when we were in a supermarket. I know she can't help it but it stops me from asking friends to call round. I daren't go to anyone else's house in case they want to come to mine. I end up staying by myself most of the time and the kids at school call me a loner.

My parents bring my sister to all my school events, but my sister shouts out a lot and I feel really embarrassed. I did try to get my mum or dad to stay at home with her but my mum got upset and said I was ashamed of my own sister. My parents argue about her a lot and I feel that they may split up if I cause a fuss. I'd talk to one of the teachers but I'm not sure my mum would like it. Have you any advice as I am feeling alone and desperate.

Yours sincerely

Jo West

(address supplied)

10.1 YEARS 7, 8 & 9 WHOLE GROUP DRAMA – PUTTING IT ALL TOGETHER

The Ballad of Charlotte Dymond by Charles Causley

It was a Sunday evening
And in the April rain
That Charlotte went from our house
And never came home again.

Her shawl of diamond redcloth
She wore a yellow gown,
She carried the green gauze handkerchief
She bought in Bodmin town.

About her throat her necklace
And in her purse her pay:
The four silver shillings
She had at Lady Day.

In her purse four shillings
And in her purse her pride.
As she walked out one evening
Her lover at her side.

Out beyond the marshes
Where the cattle stand,
With her crippled lover
Limping at her hand.

Charlotte walked with Matthew
Through the Sunday mist,
Never saw the razor
Waiting at his wrist.

Charlotte she was gentle
But they found her in the flood
Her Sunday beads among the reeds
Beaming with her blood.

Matthew, where is Charlotte,
And wherefore has she flown?
For you walked out together
And now are come alone.

Why do you not answer,
Stand silent as a tree,
Your Sunday worsted stockings
All muddied to the knee?

Why do you mend your breast-pleat
With a rusty needle's thread
And fall with fears and silent tears
Upon your single bed?

Why do you sit so sadly
Your face the colour of clay
And with a green gauze handkerchief
Wipe the sour sweat away?

Has she gone to Blisland
To seek an easier place?
And is that why your eye won't dry
And blinds your bleaching face?

'Take me home!' cried Charlotte,
'I lie here in the pit!
A red rock rests upon my breasts
And my naked neck is split!'

Her skin was soft as sable,
Her eyes were wide as day,
Her hair was blacker than the bog
That licked her life away.

Her cheeks were made of honey,
Her throat was made of flame
Where all around the razor
Had written its red name.

As Matthew turned at Plymouth
About the tilting Hoe,
The cold and cunning Constable
Up to him did go.

'I've come to take you, Matthew,
Unto the Magistrate's door.
Come quiet now, you pretty poor boy,
And you must know what for.'

'She is as pure,' cried Matthew,
'As is the early dew,
Her only stain it is the pain
That round her neck I drew!

'She is as guiltless as the day
She sprang forth from her mother.
The only sin upon her skin
Is that she loved another.'

They took him off to Bodmin,
They pulled the prison bell,
The sent him smartly up to heaven
And dropped him down to Hell.

All through the granite kingdom
And on its travelling airs
Ask which of these two lovers
The most deserves your prayers.

And your steel heart search, Stranger
That you may pause and pray
For lovers who come not to bed
Upon their wedding day.

But lie upon the moorland
Where stands the sacred snow
Above the breathing river,
And the salt sea-winds go.

FURTHER READING

Ackroyd, J (2000) *Literacy Alive*, Hodder & Stoughton

Bolton, G (1984) *Drama as Education*, Longman

Johnson, L and O'Neill, C (ed.) (1984) *Dorothy Heathcote: collected writings on education and drama*, Stanley Thornes (Publishers) Ltd

NATE Drama Committee (2000) *Cracking Drama*, NATE

Neelands, J (1992) *Learning through Imagined Experience*, Hodder & Stoughton

Neelands, J (1998) *Beginning Drama 11–14*, David Foulton Publishers

Neelands, J (1990) *Structuring Drama Work*, Cambridge University Press

O'Neill, C and Lambert, A (1984) *Drama Structures*, Hutchinson

Taylor, K (ed.) (1991) *Drama Strategies*, Heinemann